THE FIVE-HOUR WORKDAY

THE

FIVE HOUR

WORKDAY

LIVE DIFFERENTLY,
UNLOCK PRODUCTIVITY,
AND FIND HAPPINESS

―――――

STEPHAN AARSTOL

THE FIVE-HOUR WORKDAY

*Live Differently, Unlock Productivity,
and Find Happiness*

ISBN   978-1-61961-437-6   *Hardcover*

        978-1-61961-451-2   *Paperback*

        978-1-61961-436-9   *Ebook*

LIONCREST

PUBLISHING

To life, liberty, and the pursuit of happiness;

that beautiful dream

we somehow lost along the way.

CONTENTS

INTRODUCTION

———

WHAT IF I TOLD YOU THAT YOU COULD WORK FEWER HOURS and be paid the same, or even more?

What if I told you that you could give all your employees a raise for free, and they could go home early, everyday?

What if I told you that this is also the fastest way to grow your business?

I doubt you'd believe me, and I don't blame you. But here's the thing: I just did it.

At my company, Tower Paddle Boards, I made one small change in 2015 that transformed my business and my life. As a result of that change, my employees and I began to enjoy our lives in a way we never imagined possible, and we also became incredibly productive in the office.

Today, my entire team is happy, our customers are happy, and business is absolutely booming. That one small change has had an enormous, positive, and lasting impact on all of us.

So, what was the change we made?

We shortened the workday to five hours. That's it.

This sounds like a simple change, but believe me, it wasn't an easy or fast decision. It took a lifetime of paradigm-shifting experiences, along with a solid understanding of our economic past and future, before I gained the courage to bet my entire company on this experiment.

Luckily, the experiment worked. In fact, it's worked so well, and so far beyond my wildest expectations, that I feel the need to share it with you. I believe this could change your life, your company, and possibly our entire society for the better.

In this book, I'll explain how to implement a five-hour workday at your company, or at least try it as an experiment. But first, I want to explain the most important aspect of the five-hour workday: why we desperately need this, and soon. And to understand that, we'll have to go back to the beginning.

The First Two Influences: My Father and My Friend

My dad was a doctor and entrepreneur. He was an optometrist, which meant that half of his job was being a doctor, and half of his job was selling contact lenses and glasses. Going to the office and seeing him work really helped me understand what an entrepreneur was, before that word became popular.

Like many young entrepreneurs trying to create something out of nothing more than an idea, the early days were lean. For a long period of time, he didn't make much money. He earned far less than he could have made by just working for someone else, until he broke through and did very well toward the middle and end of his career.

It was that struggle and grind and payoff of entrepreneurship that really appealed to me. I watched my dad go through that transition, where he toiled for years to get his business up and running, and then grew it to the point where he was able to leap past everybody else.

Coming out of school, I knew I wanted to go into business

as an entrepreneur. Watching and understanding my dad's work inspired me to pursue this path, from a very early age.

Outside of work, my father had a relentless sense of wanderlust and a passion for ferreting out the world's best salmon fishing grounds. Family vacations were always spent in some remote campground, Indian village, or dilapidated fishing town in search of salmon all over the Pacific Northwest and Canada. There is no other way to describe my childhood memories than "wild."

We'd get lost at sea in the fog, and get caught in storms. My father would have to throw me and my two brothers upfront so we wouldn't fall overboard. There were engine failures where we'd have to limp home for hours on a trolling motor, and encounters with unidentifiable sea creatures and sea snakes, monsters really.

And there were many other adventures, whether it was the time we camped where bears would wander through our campsite, or the time when we were literally being chased by Indians with knives. It was always an adventure. The adventures that my father introduced me to were so epic that I often wonder if they really happened, or whether I dreamt them up.

Luckily, my brothers can confirm the stories, and help me to remember how much my father influenced me toward both entrepreneurship and adventure.

One Very Impactful Friend

During those same formative years of childhood, I was very lucky to have a best friend who would greatly impact the type of entrepreneur I wanted to be, and what type of life I wanted live.

My friend's name was Mason. Mason Payne.

We went to kindergarten together, and then on to first grade, and second. One day on the way home from school, while we were riding in the school bus, Mason started throwing up. I wish that was the worst part of the story, but it's not. Because he was throwing up blood.

A week later, he was diagnosed with leukemia. We were all told that Mason had, at most, a couple of years left in his short life. This was in the late 1970s, when leukemia was not very treatable.

As Mason's best friend, I was there beside him, witnessing what he was going through. He lost his hair, and the kids at school would make fun of him. It was a horrible thing to go through for him, but the way he responded to it was courageous, and very inspiring to me.

The cancer changed Mason's opinion toward what he should be doing with his remaining window of life. His attitude seemed to be this: "I've only got a couple of years to live, and I'm going to fight this thing, but I'm on the clock here. I've got to enjoy this life as much as I can, and I've got to do it right now."

That's how he operated. And luckily, I went along with him, and learned to operate the same way.

When Mason was going through his chemotherapy and cancer treatments, he would be really tired, and often couldn't make it out of bed. But when he had the energy, we were always out doing stuff. And by stuff, I mean adventures.

Mason outlived his diagnosis by several years. At one point, when we were about 10 years old, we had a BB gun war at his house. The era of the classic BB gun war is long gone now, and this is definitely not what most kids would (or should) be doing today. It's a bit insane really, that we ever did this. I have a son now, and it scares me to think of him being in a BB gun war. But this was the 1970s and 1980s, and that was a different time.

Mason's bones were very brittle at this point, and one of his legs were broken, so his brother decided to pull him around in a wagon during the BB gun war. To make it fair, it was decided that Mason would get the semi-automatic BB gun, and the rest of the neighborhood boys would get the single-shot rifles.

In the thick of battle, I got behind his mom's car, between the wheels. Mason was behind a tree, but I had a shot, and I connected. It stung him right on the neck, and I'll never forget how he came after me. It really made him mad, and he just started unloading shots at me, shooting up his mom's car in the process. I hopped up and ran toward a tree, and Mason was on the chase.

Before I made it to the tree, he'd hit me at least two or three times in the leg, yelling excitedly at his brother to pull him faster along. It was an insane experience, but it was exhilarating. We were at war. When other kids were playing with toy soldiers, Mason wanted to have an actual war. He wasn't going to live that long, so he wanted the true war adventure. And he got just that, while bringing us into his adventure too. It was a lot of fun.

Being friends with Mason was a powerful education in living presently and adventurously. He wasn't going to worry about the future, and he wasn't worried about material things like a car. He was focused on now, and the current adventure.

In Steve Jobs' famous speech to a graduating class of Stanford students, he said the following:

> Remembering that I'll be dead soon is the most important tool I've ever encountered to help me make the big choices in life. Because almost everything—all external expectations, all pride, all fear of embarrassment or failure—these things just fall away in the face of death, leaving only what is truly important.
>
> Remembering that you are going to die is the best way I know to avoid the trap of thinking you have something to lose. You are already naked. There is no reason not to follow your heart.

When I first heard that speech, where Jobs explained how his cancer diagnosis changed his perspective on life, I realized that Mason's cancer experience was equally impactful to me.

Whether the cancer is your own, or you're experiencing it vicariously through someone you really care about, it absolutely does change how you look at the world.

Another Lesson: Gratitude and Humility

There were more lessons from Mason that helped me understand how very lucky I was, at a time when I might have otherwise been less humble.

Mason was dealing with cancer, and chemotherapy, and kids making fun of him for losing his hair. Then things got worse: his dad died, in a freak accident on a three-wheeler while he was off commercial fishing in Alaska to pay the bills. So Mason had to go through that too. Then his mom re-married, and it was a tough situation to say the least.

Mason had to move schools, so he had to be the new kid with cancer, at a new school. Those kids were picking on him, knocking his crutches out from under him, and laughing as Mason fell to the ground. He had to endure this horrendous and difficult life until the day he died, at age 13.

But amazingly, his spirits were almost always positive. His resilience was a great example and inspiration to me, and was humbling at the same time. At the same time that Mason was enduring his obstacles, I was living a life that was pretty idealistic. My parents were divorced when I was about three or four years old. A few years later they both married other people, but when I was 12, they divorced those other people and re-married each other. It was a dream come true for me, at the time.

As Mason's world was falling apart, my world was coming together. My parents got back together, I was the class president of the sixth grade, I won the school's scholar athlete award that I had coveted for years, and our basketball team had a perfect season. I was having all this good fortune, while at the same time seeing all of Mason's bad fortune.

This was a lesson in resilience, gratitude, and humility. At an early age, Mason gave me a perspective on the fragility of life, and how grateful we should be for what we have. We shouldn't complain, because we actually have an extraordinarily good life, while it lasts. I think a lot of people miss that in the modern world.

When combined, these childhood lessons and perspectives taught me that the life we have is really short, but really quite good while we're alive, so we should be as present and adventurous as we can possibly be. Every single day.

That's how I started looking at life as a child, and that's how I look at it today.

Applying The Lessons I Learned From Mason

I grew up near Bellingham, Washington, in the small logging town of Deming. High school went well for me, and I assumed I would get into any college I wanted to. Because of that, I only applied to one college: Claremont McKenna, a small private school in California.

I was denied admission.

When that happened, I said screw it. I'm going on an adventure, and I'm doing it now.

The weather is pretty rainy and horrible in my hometown, so it seemed like a great idea to go live on the beach in Hawaii, and take a year off.

The term "gap year" is more commonly used now, describing what I did by taking a year off between high school and college. But in 1990, this was a very unusual thing to do in America. I was the class president, gave a speech at graduation, and everybody would ask what I was doing after high school.

I'm going to college, I told them. But first, I'm going to spend a year in Hawaii. And people didn't know how to respond to that, because it was an unusual and unnatural decision for most 18-year-olds to make, back then.

But after all those years of being influenced by Mason, it was a natural decision for me. It was natural to react to an obstacle by going on an adventure. It had become a habit to be present in the current moment, and enjoy life to the fullest, despite the uncertainty of what the future might hold.

Spending that time in Hawaii was one of the best decisions I ever made, and it began a domino effect of adventures that would teach me what life was like in other cultures around the world.

I came back from Hawaii and attended college in my hometown, at Western Washington University. I made great friends there, and I told them about the incredible time I'd spent in Hawaii. My friends got jazzed about it, to the point that they wanted to experience it for themselves.

So, after our sophomore year of college, we said screw it. Four friends and I said we're going on a six month sabbatical to Hawaii. We did the same thing I'd done right out of high school, and we had an amazing time.

As a result of the successful Hawaii trip, one of those same guys and some other friends of ours took a longer trip together, two years later. Upon graduating from college, we went on a three-month backpacking trip through Australia. Our first extended travel.

Similar to high school, a lot of classmates were asking me, "What job are you going to start after college?" As graduation got closer, everyone was trying to land a job. Everyone but us, that is.

We were planning our escape.

Opportunity Knocks, But Few Answer

When we were planning this trip, only three of us had committed to doing the trip to Australia, and we wanted a bigger group to go. The funny thing is, when we were trying to talk other people into going, their excuses revealed a lot about our society.

They'd say, wow, I'd love to do that. I wish I could. I just can't, because I have to do this or that to do, after I graduate. It was laughable. Every single time, it was something ridiculous. Something they had the rest of their lives to do.

Of course you can go, I thought. *It's not going to cost much money, because we're going to live like peasants. You don't have a job now, so you don't have to quit a job.*

But the reality is that nearly everybody had a plan of exactly what they needed to do next. The problem is that it really wasn't their plan. It was someone else's plan for them, or an unwritten societal plan that everyone was supposed to follow.

This common American plan seemed to go something like this:

1. You need to go to high school.
2. As soon as you graduate high school, you need to go immediately to college.
3. You need to finish college in four years, and then immediately get a job.

There is such an unnecessary rush to get to the point of working. A rush to steam through this plan as fast as possible, with no breaks along the way. Where did this terrible plan come from?

Seth Godin says it best in his popular TED talk "Stop Stealing Dreams," which you can find on YouTube. Our current education system, he said, was created several decades ago and had one purpose: to create a better factory worker. More compliance, more obedience, less creativity, more fear. Follow the rules, fit in, and don't even think about trying to blaze your own trail.

To me, that's where this unwritten plan comes from. It's someone else's plan, some society's plan for our lives. But it doesn't have to be that way now, if you're willing to take a mental leap of faith.

When you dismiss something just because it seems

impractical, you often miss genuine opportunities for personal and professional growth. You just have to say "yes" and take the plunge. And some chances present themselves only once.

What I Learned in Australia

We ended up with a group of four guys, and we embarked upon an epic three months in Australia. We were partying every night, chasing girls during the day, and taking adventure trips along the eastern coast of the country.

Our mode of transport was a cheap hop-on-hop-off backpacker bus that cycled back and forth from Sydney to Cairns, which is over 1,500 miles. We were surprised to meet thousands of kindred spirits just like us, on this same adventure. They were mostly from Europe, but there were also small contingencies from all over the globe. Meeting new backpackers everywhere we went would become a pattern in Australia.

We spent our three months in a consistent cycle of meeting new people and going on adventures. We would go on a three-day sailing cruise, where we'd make 15 new friends, and spend a couple of days with them. Then we would go on to the next town, where we'd meet even more new people. Some would travel ahead and we'd reconnect randomly weeks later. By the end of our journey, we would go into a random small town halfway across the world and run into old friends with alarming regularity.

It was a transformative experience for me, learning from this caravan of traveling backpackers from around the world. When I started talking to somebody new, they would never ask me, "What do you do?" That would be pointless, because nobody was working.

Instead, they'd ask, "What did you do last week? What did you do today? What are you going to do tonight? What movies do you like? What are your plans for tomorrow?" Conversations became

2. I learned that I truly cared about bringing the Aussie mindset to America. The "backpacker bus" might not have been the best way to do it, but I wanted to keep trying.

In San Diego, I had an $8/hour job at a tech company, and was bartending at night to afford my rent. After about a year of that, I was at this point where I thought, *Jesus, do I really want to be a bartender for the rest of my life?*

I still wanted to do this backpacker bus in America. It was a dream that inspired me. With that in mind, I went to grad school for an MBA at the University of San Diego. With an MBA, I knew I would make a higher salary at my day job, and possibly be able to get my own business off the ground.

I put together a business plan when I was in grad school, and decided that it would be a much better business to build hostels, instead of operating the backpacker bus. Fewer moving parts. So I set out to build a chain of resort-style youth hostels in the United States.

I met a guy whose parents had money, and he indicated that they informally agreed to put in about $500,000 toward my business plan. I did my last MBA class in Barcelona, so I could travel around Europe to interview hostel managers and owners. I was trying to recruit somebody to come back and help me run this business.

The investors' money fell through. I'd need to delay my dream once more.

A Well-Timed Economic Boom and a Monster Fish

Luckily, this was 1999, and I was in the right city to take advantage of the huge tech boom in America during that time. I went to work for a tech startup.

Since I was the young kid out of grad school, and because nobody understood the coming power of digital marketing yet, my company told me to figure out the internet marketing side of this and how to get people to our website. That's where I cut my teeth in internet marketing.

Back then, you could buy website traffic for one penny per click. We built this whole company using internet marketing, because nobody else in our industry understood the internet. But my company's founder did, our team did, and I did. And I used that skill to help grow that company for five years, but I still had an entrepreneurial bug.

I loved gambling, and I especially loved poker. As luck would have it, the poker industry absolutely skyrocketed, after an amateur poker player named Chris Moneymaker won the World Series of Poker.

People started playing poker more often with their friends, and local tournaments popped up everywhere. With the arrival of the internet, online poker became a new reality. Poker was everywhere, online and offline.

I'd gambled in Vegas enough to know that something was missing: real, authentic poker chips. So I went directly to the poker chip manufacturers, put $10,000 worth of custom poker chips on my credit card, and I started the site BuyPokerChips.com.

Six months into the venture, I got my first online order. It was Christmas Day in 2003, and it was about a $500 order. It was a merry Christmas—the first time I had sold anything!

After about another six months of moonlighting this startup around my day job, things began to really take off. It was July, and my new company was already on pace to do $50,000 in monthly sales. I soon found myself back on the Washington coast on a fishing trip with my father in a rundown Indian reservation called Neah Bay.

Neah Bay was the same town where my brother and I, as kids, had been chased down the beach by a gang of Indian kids with knives. As they began to chase us, my brother may have incited the incident when he pulled out a BB gun that had a breaking barrel, like a shotgun that pumped up the air pressure.

That's right about the time when the knives came out.

I fled down the beach, while my brother ran up an embankment lined with sharp rocks and shells and ran into the local cafe. Gun in hand and bloody feet, the cafe patrons looked up briefly then went back to eating, as if this type of thing happened every day. My brother called our dad from the pay phone inside to come and rescue him, as the child gang eyed him from outside.

Back to the fishing trip. That July evening in 2004, my father and I were out on the boat talking to my idea of quitting my day job, when my fishing pole jerked violently and line began screaming out. Twenty-five minutes of fighting that fish later, my Dad netted the biggest fish I'd ever caught in my life. It was a monster of a king salmon, and we guessed it to be around 40 pounds.

Dad thought we should take it into the marina and weigh it immediately, so we did. That salmon ended up being 49 inches long and 58.5 pounds. One of the Indian chiefs ran the marina and offered to buy it from us for $500. It was a huge fish, and typically they aren't that good to eat, so Dad and I thought about it for a while and came back with our own proposal: we'd give him the fish for free, but with two conditions. One, he had to mount it and display it on the wall inside the marina store, and two, we wanted free moorage for our boat in the marina for life. He agreed.

It was a small town. The next day was about as close to celebrity as I'd ever been. Everyone knew about the fish and that we caught it. Word filtered back that the chief would have gone as high as $5,000 for that fish. It was the biggest fish caught in the State of Washington in more than a decade.

We made the next day's newspaper in Seattle. I amused myself that it was my first Indian treaty, and it could even be considered to be reparations, since the white man got the short end of the stick for once! But I couldn't have cared less about the money, and only felt an immense gratitude for that experience.

The odds on catching that fish were literally one in a million, or even less than that. I took it as a sign that I was on a lucky streak. I emailed in my resignation a week later and I officially became an entrepreneur.

This would be a big leap of faith in any circumstance, but the stakes were higher now: my son was due to be born in five months in December. All my chips were on the table. Alex was born on December 7th.

That month, my business would do more than $140,000 in sales—my biggest month ever—and I'd pocket more in that one month than my day job paid me in an entire year. By 2005 I had a business pulling in $500,000 a year. I would pocket a little over $100,000 of that, which was nice.

But there was a problem: it was consuming my entire life. And that's when another stroke of luck happened for me.

A Book That Changed My World

During that same time, a guy named Tim Ferriss wrote a book about automation, leverage, and working to live. The book was called *The Four Hour Workweek*, and it changed many people's lives, including mine.

I bought a bunch of copies of that book, gave them to all of my friends, and told them, "You've got to see this. This guy is on to something here. The world has changed."

Tim's book is loaded with valuable ideas that helped me leverage my time, toward living the life I wanted to live. The book is still relevant today, and I highly recommend reading it if you haven't already.

At that point in my poker chip business, I was a one-man show. I had this business that was generating half a million a year in revenue, and it was all me. I was the guy on the phone, the guy who shipped the stuff, the graphic designer, the website guy, the marketing guy, and the accountant. Everything.

I was working a full week, but it wasn't making me any more money. So, I began applying one of Tim's most powerful ideas: management by absence. Stop doing tasks you believe are essential, and see what happens.

First, I stopped shipping every day. I started shipping only on Monday, Wednesday, and Friday. I thought I'd try that and see if customers complained. There was no change. Nobody complained.

Next, I applied it to the phone. I stopped answering the phone on Tuesdays and Thursdays. Again, no change, and no complaints.

Wow, I thought. *I just freed up two entire days of the week. This is amazing.*

I applied that concept to every aspect of my business, and in the end, my 40-hour workweek became a 12-hour workweek. My life was changed, and my time was free for other ventures.

With my newly free schedule, I spent three or four years trying different businesses, and failing with all of them. I tried a toy company, a drink token company, and a green energy company, among others. Nothing was really breaking through and taking off, like the poker chips had.

Then I got lucky again, in a way that brings this story full circle.

Adventures Old and New

Remember that college trip to Australia? Well, one of my buddies from that trip came to visit me in San Diego. He was still a very adventurous guy, and he would always push me to try new things.

On this particular visit, he was able to convince me to get out of bed at 5:30 a.m. and head down to La Jolla Shores to try something I never would've tried otherwise: stand up paddle surfing.

It was also strikingly beautiful, before most people were even up, with the sun just over the lush hills of La Jolla. I was wondering why everyone doesn't enjoy this. In a city of nearly three million people, only a handful of people enjoy this experience. It's right here for the taking, and it's free.

I love traditional surfing, but surfing is a lot more difficult than it looks. It's tough to catch waves, and takes a ton of energy and swimming. But when my buddy took me out into the ocean on a paddle board, I started catching every single wave, after only 20 minutes of learning to balance myself on this new type of board.

This paddle surfing was so much easier. I'll never forget how there was a 65-year-old guy out there doing it, and he was kind of out of shape, but catching as many waves as a professional surfer.

"Hey man, you're pretty good!" I yelled over. "How long have you been doing this?"

"Thanks!" he yelled back. "It's only my fifth day!"

I was absolutely shocked.

Then I got stung. I fell off the board and stepped on what felt like a sharp rock. I look at my foot and it looked like someone sliced a quarter inch gash with a sharp knife. It's bleeding and throbbing a bit. Feeling like a bit of a candy ass, I tell my friend I think I've got to get out and take care of this. It starts throbbing more.

I start running toward the lifeguard tower about a quarter mile away. The throbbing started to run up my leg into my inner thigh. I was getting a little freaked out, as the increase in blood flow by running seemed to be accelerating this thing.

I slowed to a walk. I was thinking I got stung by a stingray or a jellyfish. I seemed to recall that you're supposed to pee on it if you get stung. As I was contemplating the pros and cons of peeing on myself right there on the beach, I asked a local surfer and he confirmed that I got hit by a sting ray.

"That's just really bad luck," he told me, before instructing me to put my foot in really hot water. It was early in the morning and the lifeguards weren't there, and there was no hot water faucet in sight. So I bailed on surfing for the day and headed home for hours of excruciating pain and recovery.

That day of paddle boarding was memorable and fun. I took the stingray incident as another sign, albeit a slightly more painful one. It was bad luck, perhaps, but really that's just all in how you look at things.

I bought a paddle board the next week, and went out on Mission Bay with my five-year-old son. He could ride up front, while I was on the back, and it was such a fun experience. I was getting an hour's exercise on this thing, and he was having a blast, fully entertained on the front of this board.

Here's where it gets even better: two or three days later, my five-year-old son is riding the board *himself.*

I started putting all these pieces together, thinking, *Wow... 5 years old, or 65 years old... both mastering it and enjoying it in a matter of hours. You can do this in the surf. You can do it in flat water. You can get exercise. This is actually a much bigger industry than people realize.*

The reality is that paddle boarding is like a combination between kayaking and surfing. It's got the cool, soulful appeal of surfing, but then it's got this adventurous appeal of kayaking. There's a fitness element to it too. I sensed it was going to be a huge industry.

All In: Betting My Chips on One Strong Hunch

The poker chip business was starting to decline, to the point where I was seriously thinking of getting a day job. I had a hunch that a paddle board company was a better bet now, so I sold my remaining inventory of my best-selling poker chip line, about $30,000 worth, and did not reinvest it in the poker chip business. I knowingly killed about 40% of my poker chip business overnight.

I took that $30,000 and started Tower Paddle Boards.

This was 2010, and the new company wasn't taking off very fast. So by January of the following year, I was actually job hunting. It was the recession, and I couldn't find a job. I was overqualified for everything I applied for, but still couldn't talk people into hiring me.

Then in about March of that year, I started to see a little trickle of sales occurring on my paddle board website. Given how poorly my job interviews were going, I thought a trickle of sales was enough to validate this market. So I bet all my poker chips on this idea, and innovated further.

There were 80 companies in this industry at this point, and it was already getting crowded. But everybody else was selling through the traditional three-tier distribution channels: brand to distributor, then to wholesaler, then to retailer. That's why these relatively inexpensive paddle boards had a high cost to the end consumer, in the range of $1,200-$1,500. It was insane.

So I changed the distribution channel of the industry, by going direct to consumers. I created my own boards, designed in San Diego and manufactured in China at the same factories that the rest of the industry was making their boards at. We sold them direct, however, at nearly half the price of boards sold in retail stores.

It went so well that we pre-sold the first shipping container of boards, before they even landed on American soil. There was most certainly a demand for these, at a lower price.

Things were starting to take off, so I hired my first employee. I explained that the company was starting to take off, but this isn't really necessarily a full time job. You've got about six months, and if you can be productive enough to pay for yourself in six months, then you'll have a full time job.

I now had myself, and one part-time employee. That's how small my Tower Paddle Board company was, when I got the call that would change everything.

Swimming With Sharks

"We'd like you to be on our show," the guy said, on the other end of the telephone.

This should be comical, I thought. *Who would want to have my little company on their show? Public access television, maybe?*

"It's called *Shark Tank.*"

I hadn't heard of this show, to be honest. And a title like *Shark Tank* sounded like a small local show. Maybe it was about surfing? But I didn't have very long to think about it, before he uttered the words that would perk me up faster than a triple espresso.

"It's on ABC. On Friday nights."

What? Was this guy serious? I couldn't believe my ears.

My initial thoughts were funny and short-sighted, in retrospect. Since my business relied heavily on search engines like Google, and links to my website were a big part of driving traffic, I remember that my first thought was: *Holy cow, I could get a link from ABC.com. That would be huge!*

I bet I'm the first person to ever go on that show, thinking more about getting internet links than funding. But then I started thinking about all the other possibilities, as well as the risks of going on the show.

At the time, I was really focused on just building the business and wasn't actively thinking about raising money. But for a chance to go on the biggest TV show in America on Friday nights and potentially get a large infusion of cash? I'd be crazy not to.

But then again, it was reality television, and I had absolutely no desire to potentially humiliate myself. So then I started thinking that it might be equally crazy to attempt this.

But just like that college trip to Australia, sometimes

opportunity only knocks once. Sometimes, if you really want to live this life to its fullest, you have to take the plunge.

So that's what I did.

Six weeks later, I'm in Los Angeles to present my business pitch on the show. Two days before filming, I learn that Mark Cuban is going to be on the show for the first time ever this upcoming season, as a "guest shark." When they told me that, I knew he'd be the guy I really wanted to focus on.

The Big Day: My Worst Fears Come True

When the moment arrived, I was actually remarkably calm. Standing backstage, looking at the monitor of the set with my board and logo in the center, I felt a sense of calm satisfaction wash over me. I was a little nervous, but at the same time I was thinking, *Wow, this is remarkable that my little company and that little logo that didn't exist just a year ago are about to be on TV in front of millions, and I'm going to pitch these Sharks.*

I was thinking, *Whatever happens out there, you know what? You've really already won. How many people really ever get an experience like this? I'm on a Hollywood movie set, seeing how all this TV business works. How fortunate am I?* After I realized that, I was as relaxed as I've probably even been in my life.

Perhaps that was a mistake.

By the time it was my turn to go on, I'd been standing around the studio all day, but I was expected to walk in there on a moment's notice and pitch these sharks, without ever having met them. It was absolutely nerve-racking.

I had a slide show of four or five slides, and I'd practiced my pitch a million times. The moment neared, and at this point, it was almost my turn. They were about to open the doors and let me walk in.

Then, just before the doors open, a producer walked up, handed me a clicker to run the slideshow, and hurriedly gave me some instructions on how to use it. I was totally confused and thrown off.

Then the doors opened.

I walked in, half looking back, thinking, "Really? You had to do that at the last minute? I've been here all day!" About 30 seconds into my pitch, I hit a button on the clicker to start my slide show. Apparently it was the wrong button to hit, because it shot through all the slides at once and landed on my final slide.

I tried to backtrack. Nothing was going right. I lost my train of thought and forgot my memorized three-minute spiel. *Oh shit*, I thought. *Oh shit.*

And that's when I froze.

My pitch is known infamously as the worst pitch ever in the history of *Shark Tank* that still ended up getting a deal. If you Google "worst pitch ever on *Shark Tank*," you'll probably find it. And it was worse than what they showed on TV, which was an edited-down version of the full calamity that took place.

It was beyond uncomfortable, and humiliating. I had to start my speech over again and try to talk through it. I was doing this very robotic thing, where I would just freeze up and be silent. And then they started making fun of me. All the sharks were just piling on the ridicule.

It was my worst nightmare. It was a very surreal moment, where I was almost looking at this from outside my body, thinking, *What are you doing down there? This is going to be on live TV. Your son is going to be so embarrassed. His friends are going to be making fun of him at school because his dad's an idiot. Pull yourself together.*

I started to explain: here's what the paddle board company is, and here's why this is a hot industry. Three of the sharks were immediately out. Barbara called me a nerd, and she called me a leprechaun. I thought there would be a bidding war, since my company was already successful. I was dead wrong.

This was the worst possible scenario I could imagine. But I've been there before.

The Time We Almost Died in Mexico (And Loved It)

One of the best things you learn when you travel, is that sometimes everything goes wrong, and that it's okay. In fact, it might even become your best memory of the trip.

On one of my adventures, my friends and I were driving across the Mexican Baja. A torrential downpour came out of nowhere, and we came upon a washed out bridge. I'm sick in the truck bed in the back, already miserable from having some kind of stomach bug.

My buddy was driving, and we're all looking at this newly-formed raging river, cascading off about a 15 foot cliff just feet beyond where we are seemingly supposed to drive. It's pouring outside and we're sitting there with a handful of other vehicles for about a half an hour, and it's just getting worse.

One heavy utility truck decides to go across and they make it. We're inspired. Then a crappy old Datson 280z starts going across and their rear-end starts sliding out just as they reach the other side. They escaped by a narrow margin.

Now we could have waited out the storm, but that may have taken a couple hours. Our truck is a pretty lightweight truck with no weight in the backend aside from me and some luggage. After debate among the group, we decide to go for it. I don't even want to drive my own car so my buddy does it and we make it across, and proceeded on our way west to Ensenada to continue our Spring Break trip. A bunch of cars are still back on the other side and presumably are going to wait it out.

Sitting there while the road was washing out, our options were to wait until it completely washed out and we have to backtrack around the long way for a couple of extra days, or we could risk life and limb by shooting across. This all seemed like incredibly bad luck, and was definitely the most unbearable point of that entire trip.

And yet, to this day, we reminisce fondly about how we almost died in this Mexican river from nowhere. Why is that?

Once you've traveled a lot, you learn that you can flip the script when bad stuff happens. After enough of this bad stuff has happened to you, and you've survived it and looked back and laugh at it all, you realize that you can actually enjoy bad things while they're happening. Why? Because you know it's going to be the greatest part of the story.

You can spin bad experiences into good things, and I guess I've learned to do that as an entrepreneur too. So that's what I did on *Shark Tank*.

The Pivot

At some point, I was able flip a switch in my mind. I calmed down and thought to myself, *look, I'm as smart as any of these guys up here. Who cares if you fell apart. Fight back and do this. This is just all going to be a footnote in the future of what happens here, so get on with it.*

And I did just that. I switched my strategy. And truthfully, I got a little angry.

I said, obviously, you guys don't get the paddle boarding thing. But what I'm trying to show you here is that I'm one of the best internet marketers you'll ever meet. I can do this for any company. I can do this for any of your companies. Heck, why don't we just buy a $10 million company, we'll inject what I know, grow the business, and sell it for $30 million? We'll just keep flipping businesses, making millions.

I was no longer pitching the paddle board company. I was pitching me.

That started some conversation. They edited all of this out from the actual episode, because I was getting very technical with my explanations of how I could do this for any company.

Cuban, being very tech-savvy, realized that I was on to something. I think he started to realize that he could possibly use me for other things, regardless of how profitable the paddle board company would become.

He offered me $150,000 for 30% of the company. Ugh. That was 20% more of my company than I wanted to give away. But it's what he wanted in addition to a share of Tower, that spoke volumes about how much he believed in me.

He said that he wanted the first right or refusal to invest in any business I raised money for in the future. He wanted the chance to be part of not just Tower Paddle Boards, but also my future ventures. This was a first in the history of *Shark Tank*.

How could I say no to that? So I didn't. And that's how Mark Cuban became my business partner.

Buckle Your Seat Belts and Prepare For Takeoff

In 2011, the year Cuban signed on, we did about $250,000 in sales.

The next year? $1.3 million.

Then, in 2013, we hit $3.1 million. Then $5 million in 2014. In 2015 we did $7.2 million. And now, in 2016, we're on pace to do about $10 million. It's been a rocket ship, and a really fun ride. I believe we would've gotten there without *Shark Tank*, but being on that show made it happen two or three years faster.

With that growth in 2014, we were invited to an event in San Diego, to celebrate the city's fastest growing private companies. There were 100 companies there, and they were counting down from the 100th fastest-growing company to the number one fastest-growing company. They were the types of companies you'd expect: startup tech companies, venture-backed companies, seasoned technology companies, and some serious heavyweight industries.

We didn't know where we were going to end up on the list.

We thought maybe we'd crack the top ten, because we knew our growth rate was astronomical. But by the time they announced the number three company, we hadn't been called. Then number two was called.

It wasn't us.

Holy crap, I thought. *We just won this thing.*

We were named the Fastest Growing Company in San Diego, and I wasn't even remotely prepared to walk up there and give a speech. I was the only guy at this event who wasn't wearing a suit. I get up on the stage, said a quick thanks, and said a few other things I don't remember. But I do remember that I said something that absolutely shocked everyone.

"My whole team is here," I said. "There's only five of us."

Everybody in the audience started looking at each other, in a way that said, "What? Did I hear that right? Five people are generating $5 million and growing like crazy? And it's a surf company. What the hell is going on here?"

That's when everyone in the room started to understand what I already knew: this game has changed.

The Opportunity to Do Something Revolutionary

Soon after the San Diego event, we were nominated to the Inc. 500 list of Fastest Growing Companies. We were the 239th fastest-growing company in the nation, according to that list.

This is the moment I realized that we had a huge opportunity in front of us. Do we want to become a 10 million dollar paddle board company, or do we want to become a 100 million dollar company that is the world's premiere beach lifestyle brand?

The $100 million company, for sure.

So, in order to accomplish that, what do we need to change? What do great brands do differently, to grow into that competitive advantage?

The answer, ultimately, was the five-hour workday. It took

our company to the next level, and it changed all of our lives for the better.

The remaining pages explain how I discovered the five-hour workday, why I trusted it, how we implemented it, and why I believe it's the perfect solution for the new world we find ourselves in.

Why The Five-Hour Workday Works in The "New Economy"

I had a hunch that this would work, in part, because I understand what some people are calling the "new economy." There's a new economic environment, and technological capabilities that empower it, being used by some of the smartest entrepreneurs in the world.

There's one goal, in this new economy: maximize your dollars earned per hour. And I'm talking about doing this to an extreme level, like the way I reduced my hours in my poker chip business from 40 hours a week to 12 hours a week. A 70% reduction for me, and for some talented entrepreneurs, a 100% reduction. They were removing themselves entirely from their businesses.

The new economy is a game of efficiency, and hundreds of thousands of smart people are playing that game right now. This includes your employees, whether you know it or not. And if one employee can do it, then an entire company can do it too, if the same mindset and tactics are leveraged.

How Much More Productive Are We Now?

Let's talk productivity and macroeconomics. According to the U.S. Bureau of Labor Statistics, business sector output has increased nine-fold since 1947, but the hours that generated that product only doubled. Hours didn't go up nine-fold. That's a massive, consistent productivity gain.

But to understand what's more relevant now, you'll have to take a look at what just happened to us, during The Great Recession.

Productivity, output, and hours worked: before, during, and after the Great Recession, fourth quarter 2006–fourth quarter 2013

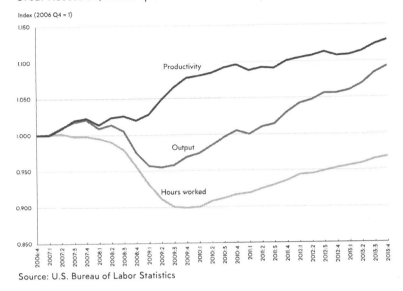

Source: U.S. Bureau of Labor Statistics

Technically, the Great Recession occurred from December 2007 to January of 2009, but if you look at the chart above, you'll see how this recession created a new productivity level that is still with us today.

If you were in America during this time, you probably felt the effects of what this chart illustrates, especially from 2007 to 2009. Everything crashed, and when that happened, people lost their jobs and working hours. That's what the bottom line shows.

But what happened when your teammate at work got let go? Did that person's duties and workload go away?

You already know the answer to that, especially if you were one of the millions of people in this situation. Of course that workload didn't go away. People were getting laid off, and the "lucky" survivors just got all of that work piled onto them, along with the new work that would come in.

Less people, more work. That's what those top two lines in the chart illustrate.

Take a closer look at the fourth quarter of 2008, all the way to the fourth quarter of 2009. Hours crashing, productivity going up. Those four quarters in America were the highest level of productivity in *35 years*.

And what happened as we came out of the recession, when the employment rate and total hours started to recover? Even more productivity gains. And those gains are never going away, because the technologies that drive this productivity are here to stay.

And what have wages done? We all know that answer. They're stagnant. So what do the smartest employees do, to raise their hourly wage? They reduce their hours, and achieve the same or higher output.

And it's never been easier to do that, in the history of the world. Especially since the world had Ferriss' book, *The Four Hour Workweek*, to show them exactly how to do it. That book came out in April of 2007, and it took the entrepreneurial world by storm, during a time when we were all trying to skyrocket our productivity just to survive.

And as you can tell by the chart, lots of people did exactly that. We have entered a new level of productivity, and it's here to stay. It will continue to take less and less hours to achieve the same output. That's a big part of why the five-hour workday is possible, and why it works.

But there's more to this story. Next, we'll take a look at things from the vantage point of our country's history, your current work role, and the entire world's future.

Who Can Benefit From Reading This Book?

There are many different types of people who can benefit from the concepts we're going to discuss. First, let's talk about how employees will benefit from reading this book.

In the last 40 years, productivity has just exploded—in the

range of 80 percent—and yet wages and benefits have gone up only about 11 percent. That's less than inflation. This is exactly what's happening, in the separation of classes and wealth. The word billionaire, that's the new millionaire. Most of the productivity gains are being sent straight to the top, to the owners of firms and the super wealthy.

Companies are becoming highly automated, and highly leveraged. They're needing fewer and fewer employees, and they're able to replace full-time workers with part-time workers at a much lower cost.

But this isn't from losing your job to someone overseas, or any other of the fear-mongering excuses you hear from politicians. Maybe they don't really want you to know why you're losing your job, or why you're not getting raises. But I'm here to tell you: it's technology and productivity. That's what's eliminating jobs, and stagnating wages.

A five-hour workday is a renegotiation of sorts. It's employees getting their fair share of our gains from productivity. Whereas before, the owners of companies just said okay, we have all this new productivity, we're going to take all of that profit, pass very little of it on to the workers, and the workers need to keep working the same hours.

But increasingly, in the new economy, employees are wanting to take back their time. To the younger generations especially, life is about much more than making money. It's about having time to do the things you love. To spend it with the people you love.

That's what the five-hour workday is about. It's about being more productive, in a way where everybody benefits. Because truthfully, we can now get done in two to three hours, what once took us eight to ten hours.

If you're an employee right now, this is how you should look at your employer and your life. And if you're reading this book, you probably are already thinking about your work in this way.

Employers Will Benefit Too

When I tell employers and business owners about the five-hour workday, their first reaction is often the traditional one that you'd expect: if the employees are winning, then the employer is losing. This traditional, outdated mindset is that it's a battle, and zero-sum game.

Not in the new economy, my fellow business owners. The world is different now. Thanks to technological advances, we are leaving behind the age of scarcity and rapidly entering an age of abundance, which I'll talk about later.

The traditional employer mindset, still lingering from the industrial age, is that less hours means less output. If someone works four hours instead of eight, they'll only get half of their work done. But what employers are failing to see is, cheats have already been worked into the system here. They're making productivity gains every day, but they're not telling you.

What are they doing instead? Facebook. Fantasy football. Amazon shopping. Vacation planning. Do I need to keep going? We all know there's a ton of waste in the typical workday. Do you know what the biggest online shopping day of the year is? It's Cyber Monday, a day where everyone is "working." Why don't employers care? Because output isn't down. Productivity isn't down.

What is down, however, are the total number of hours we need to do our work.

That's part of where telecommuting comes from. It's from employees who understand that they need to get the hell out of the office, because they really only need two or three hours a day to get all of their work done. And now we've got a huge growth in freelance workers, and employees choosing to go to that side of the table, for (what I believe to be) the same reasons.

The writing is on the wall, and employers just need to wake up to this reality.

If you're an employer, and you agree with me that your most talented and productive workers are going to be hard to retain in the future ahead of us, then you ought to be thinking about how to compete in that environment. An environment where workers are looking to make the same (or more) money, in fewer hours.

In the knowledge worker sector, it's a race for talent. In my company and industry, I'd say that one brilliant, innovative, productive employee is worth 3 to 5 average employees. I'm betting it's that way in your business too, and maybe even exponentially more important than it is in mine.

And you know what? The brilliant people, they know they're brilliant, and more productive than everyone around them. That's why they leave for more money, or fewer hours. That's why they start their own business, or go to the freelancing side of the table.

So how do you attract and retain these talented people? You've got to give them a new bargain. As they say in the entrepreneurial world, you've got to figure out how to "expedite the inevitable." Be in front of the curve, or become a victim of it.

That's what the five-hour workday is. You're saying, "Look, I'm going to give you a big part of your life back. It's going to be the same money you'd make at an eight-hour-a-day competitor of ours, but you'll only need to be here five hours a day."

The average worker in America actually works 47 hours a week, not 40. In fact, 25 percent of people report that they work more than sixty hours a week, and another 25 percent work around 50 hours a week. So, almost half of America is working 50 hours a week or more.

This is an epidemic, and it's going to correct itself. And if you want be ahead of the curve, and you want to attract those talented people instead of lose them, then you're reading the right book.

When you cut a fair bargain like this one, and give employees the respect and freedom that they deserve, you'll not only retain your own talent, but you'll start stealing talent from everybody else in town. In the next few years—and the next few decades, perhaps—this strategy will have massive benefits in recruitment and hiring, for every company that offers a shorter workday.

This can also bolster customer loyalty and your overall sales. When your end customers see and hear how well your employees are treated (because you should be talking about this on social media, in a way that customers can see it), that's going to build brand equity and goodwill. Customers are employees somewhere too, after all, and thus tend to buy products and services from companies that take good care of their employees.

And your employees, being happy, will have happier interactions with your end customers. Happy employees, happy customers. Isn't this what we all want?

But What If I'm a Retail Business?

We have a retail store, for Tower. We reduced that to a five-hour workday as well. You know what happened? Nothing. The hours are posted on our website, and we get the same number of people coming to the store. They just come during a smaller window of time.

But What If I'm a Telephone-Based Business?

We have to maintain a customer service aspect to our business, and talk with customers via phone. We took this down to a five-hour workday too. We posted the new customer service call center hours on the website.

Did anything change? No. Were there customer complaints? Not one.

Again, the fears I had toward eliminating some of these hours, they were just that: fears. My fears did not become reality.

The reality is this: your customers will adjust. What does it matter if your hours are five hours a day, or eight hours a day? It doesn't matter at all, as long as they know you're available at some time, and that their experience is a pleasurable one when it happens.

But What If I'm in Logistics/Warehouses/Shipping?

We have a warehouse. This was a tougher challenge, because they really were putting in more than five hours a day of labor. But it wasn't as efficient and productive as it could've been, so the five-hour workday forced them to innovate.

That's the beauty of the new economy: there are technologies for nearly every problem. For warehouses, it's software. When you try to do things faster, you look past all of the artificial constraints, and only then can you see something like we found. Software that eliminated many tasks that added labor hours.

This is why bootstrapped startups often outperform huge corporations with a ton of money. Startups don't have money to throw at problems, so they must innovate. And when they do, it eliminates the problem that needed money to fix. Mark Cuban is constantly telling me this. When I tell him we have cash flow problems, he says, listen. Everybody has cash flow problems. Get over it. You need to figure out ways around that, and when you do, it will actually be your strength.

When you've got plenty of hours to do your job, and twice as much time to get the work done, then who cares how the factory is laid out? Who cares about software? You just throw man hours at things and don't look for hacks. You become a non-competitive, non-creative company.

This is why private enterprise almost always outperforms governmental agencies that basically have unlimited funds because they can just raise revenue (taxes). The constraints of "profit or die" forces private companies to become efficient with both money and people. Remove those constraints entirely, and the efficiency optimization of labor and money goes out the window.

Most people today intrinsically understand this with money, because they've been witness to the waste omnipresent in governmental budgets. But the massive human productivity wastes are harder to perceive.

That's the problem that the five-hour workday solves. When we went to the five-hour workday in the warehouse, all of the sudden, we had to figure out how to do it all in five hours. It forced us to do stuff that we should have already been doing, but had no incentive to.

The Benefits to Families and Children

If you want to look at an absolute crisis in America, look at what's happening to family time.

Fifty years ago, when we had a middle class and people didn't work 50+ hours per week, we had a strong family atmosphere with plenty of time to be with your family. Time for family dinners, extracurricular activities, community events, and all the other aspects of human life that are healthy.

Then, a decade or two later, the cost of living started to rise, and wages didn't rise with it. Soon, every family needed both parents to work. The mother and father work, the kids are in school. The kids are getting off school at 2:30 in the afternoon and the parents are still working until 5:00 at night. Less family time, and more expense on daycare.

Then go forward another decade or two, to today. Cost of living and raising children is outrageously expensive, and still, wages remain the same. No more "home at 5 o'clock," either. Half of America isn't home until 7:00 p.m. Less family time, more daycare expense. Or evening care, it should be called!

It's just getting insane. And you know who pays the biggest price of all? The kids. Our future.

In 2013, the organization UNICEF did a comprehensive

study of children's happiness and wellbeing, in the 29 most developed countries in the world. The United States finished 26th. Fourth *worst*.

I say it once again: our culture has reached a crisis level of unhappiness and wellness. And it doesn't need to be that way. We can make choices to reverse this.

I'm a father, and I'm experiencing the reversal of this in my life, with my son. I have extra time in my life now, since I'm off at 1:00 p.m., and when he's with me, it's 100% dad and son time. He gets all of my attention and energy.

When he has a baseball game at 4:00 p.m., I'm there. And I'm rested, so I have the energy to be engaged. I'll go to practices sometimes just for the joy of watching my son play. For the first time in my life, coaching is an option now too, if I so desire.

I run one of the fastest-growing companies in the country with a tiny team. I'm committed to making it the biggest beach lifestyle company in the world. Yet, I can coach little league on the side if I so desire. It's hard to say that for a lot of high-performing people in today's business environment.

Now imagine what our country would look like, and how happy our children and families might be, if every parent was home a little after 1:00 p.m., before their kids were even done with school. How would your life be different, if that was you and your family?

It's now possible to make that vision a reality.

Closing The Gender Gap, The Easy Way

Gender is a very complicated subject, but one thing is for certain: women face all kinds of terrible decisions that their male counterparts don't have to make, when it comes to their careers. And there's no shortage of data when it comes to showing the historical discrepancy in pay, although that trend has been reversing in younger generations.

The women I know who are mothers, the thing they seem to care about most is the quality of life for their children. How many women in this country feel like they need to leave their 50+ hour a week job, just to give their children a good quality of life?

How many women have their earning power knocked down, and kept down, when they take a few years off to do that? Or even if they're just taking a few afternoons off per week?

How many employers out there treat women differently, and pay them less, because of an assumption that they'll be leaving the workforce at some point to care for children? Or an assumption that mothers won't be able to work past 6:00 p.m. because they actually care about being part of their children's lives?

Can you see how a five-hour workday would help (or end) every single one of those problems? I can.

Defining Ourselves on Our Own Terms (Not By Our Job Titles)

When I travelled in Australia, it was a very friendly atmosphere, and felt like a cozy pub culture, everywhere. Everybody would get off work at a reasonable hour, and many would go to the local pub. You'd have a prominent politician sitting beside a guy off the street, right at the bar, talking happily. There was no separation of classes, like we have in America.

I believe that the closer you can get to a class-free society, the closer you're going to get to defining yourself by the things that actually drive happiness. When you define yourself by job titles, or power, or money, that all boils down to one thing: work. You're living to work.

But when you define yourself by your interests, your travels, and your communities, then you're *working to live*. The point of work becomes to make enough money to live a good life, a life with presence and time. Work exists to enable that life.

But these past few decades, our culture has twisted you into thinking that your value is defined by your work. You're defined by what you do for work, how much money you make, and the possessions you buy with that money.

The beach lifestyle people, the audience of people we serve at Tower, they reject all of that. They'd much rather live in a shack at the beach, than a mansion in the hills. The beach lifestyle people will take the part-time job, and take less money, so they can live the life they want to live.

But it doesn't have to be less money anymore. A five-hour workday is about being more productive, receiving the same or better pay, and getting your life back. It's a life that is better than most people's vacation days, which seem to start in late morning or early afternoon anyways.

Well, you'll have those same hours and free time, every single day. And you'll have them filled with the things and people you love. And unlike vacation, these days will never end.

What You'll Get From Reading This Book

I took the time to create this book, in large part, because I want to help people think differently about how we're living and working. The most helpful way to read this book will be to look at your life, and what is possible, with a completely blank slate.

If you want a life that is different from the masses, then you truly must live and work differently. When you figure out ways to do that, it's then that you'll encounter the best opportunities in life and business.

We've been completely railroaded. Our society's corporations and institutions have driven us down a path that really wasn't our choice, when it comes to working for 40 hours (or more) every week.

Most people just assume that's how it's always been, but that's not true. This was essentially invented in 1938, and put into law and cultural norms. It's only been around for 80 years, which isn't very long, in the larger history of America and humanity in general.

In addition, most people assume that it's normal in most of the world's developed countries, to work 40 hours per week. But it's not. There is no normal. Some countries are working 30 hours a week, while some are logging 60 hours a week, and their societies and lives are very different as a result. The ironic thing is that the societies working the most hours are actually the least well off, when it comes to quality of life and the amount of money they earn.

In Part One of this book, we'll dive deeper into those two mysteries—why Americans are currently working eight hours a day, and how other countries are different—because understanding the past and present is absolutely critical to understanding how we can transition into a better future.

In Part Two, we'll take a look at how our world has dramatically changed, with the advent of the internet. We all know that the world has been changing, and fast. But what's less obvious is what we can do with these new capabilities, at work and at home.

We'll look at all the reasons that the current eight-hour day is now outdated and unnecessary. Then, we'll go back to the drawing board. We'll start from scratch, and design a way of working that will be better for all of us.

In Parts Three and Four, we'll dig into the specifics of exactly how we implemented a five-hour workday at Tower Paddle Boards, and the many benefits we're experiencing. We'll talk conceptually about how you could apply some of what we've learned to your business, and hopefully, toward enriching your personal life.

Lastly, in Part Five, we'll hop inside my time machine and head to the future. I'll show you what will be possible next, and how our lives could be better than anything we've ever imagined.

And by the end of the book, I think you'll be ready to join me in the final piece of the puzzle: action. Because we all know that it's time for a change.

So let's be that change.

PART I

—

THE FASCINATING HISTORY OF WORK

Chapter One

THE AGRICULTURAL AGE: BEFORE AND AFTER

Working to Live (and Survive) in the Stone Age

How much did humans work in the stone age, and why?

Stone age tribes didn't distinguish between work and leisure like we do today. They didn't even have words in their language to explain the difference between work and leisure.

Interestingly, this is how I feel entrepreneurs look at the world, when they really love what they're doing. Richard Branson, one of today's prominent thought leaders on entrepreneurship and happiness, once said, "I don't think of work as work and play as play. It's all living."

It's a bit funny to me, that if we're successful at finding our passion in the modern world, our reward is that we get to experience the happiness of a caveman. I don't think many of us would choose to go back to the stone age, but let's look at their working lives.

In the stone age, work could be summarized by the word "providing." Every day, for about three hours a day, adults did the necessary hunting and foraging that would keep them alive for the remainder of the day (or maybe even the next day, if they were lucky).

There are two aspects of this that are interesting to me:

1. **Fewer hours of work.** Their daily three hours of work is a very small number, and only 21 hours of work per week, when compared to our eight-hour day and 40 hours per week.
2. No rules. There were no rules on what they were doing with their lives, and how they chose to work and find food. They did what they wanted with their time, and they worked only to find the energy to keep doing what they wanted.

Ancient Greece: A Relatively Sophisticated Period in World History

Let's hop forward in time to the first organized societies, and more specifically, the ancient Greeks. What was life about, and what was the purpose of work, to this famous and glorified society?

The Greeks actually looked at work as a curse. The Greek word for work is *ponos*, and it's derived from the Latin word *poena*, which means "sorrow."

Intelligent people during that time didn't work. Now, slavery enabled much of this, which is of course a terrible thing. But the point is that most people didn't work, at least in the way we think of work today.

If the ancient Greeks lived in America today, most people here would consider them bums. It would be widely assumed that these people were lazy, and not contributing to our society. It certainly would not be an aspirational story from a parent to a child, to become such a person.

But in ancient Greece, it truly *was* aspirational to avoid work. If you needed to work, you were not considered successful.

Compare this to America today. People define themselves by what they do for work. People work nights and weekends, and often wear it like a badge of honor, to be a "hard worker." And yet, they hate their jobs and can't wait for the weekend.

What changed, between this Greek culture and ours today?

Over the next thousand years, not much would change. Work was just a means to an end, and viewed as a necessary evil in many ways. During the time of the ancient Greeks, and for a thousand years after them, it was understood that work was not the most important thing to do with your life.

What was more important than work? Reading. Philosophy. Travel. Art. Community. Family. The enriching aspects of life that we don't have time for anymore, because we're working all day and night.

Pre-Industrial Europe: Where Enlightenment Died

In the sixteenth century there was a religious and political upheaval in Europe.

As part of the chaos of that time, the religious and political forces began to impose their agenda into every aspect of human life, especially the role and purpose of working.

I'll stop short of calling this abusive, but I will call it this: brainwashing. These institutions and their leaders began to brainwash people into believing that work was a good thing. Work builds character, and is holy. Work will get you into heaven. And who doesn't want to go to heaven?

Work was re-branded, and re-positioned as ethical. Work was good for the soul. Work kept your hands from being idle, and idle hands, they insisted, would lead to doing the work of the devil. That would be a surefire path to hell, and who wants to spend eternity in hell?

Take note that these ideas were all just made up by men and women no different than you or me, except for the fact that they were perhaps in a position of power at the time. They just decided that work was no longer a curse—but rather, a blessing and a virtue—because that served their purposes and their agenda.

They decreed that everyone go along with this, and entire societies changed as a result.

German sociologist Max Weber, centuries later, would research the profound impact of religions on economics and cultures around the world. When looking at this period in pre-industrial Europe, he coined a phrase that you've possibly heard: "Protestant work ethic."

Weber noted that, for a person to acquire this new, religion-driven status, they'd need to achieve the following attributes: diligence, punctuality, deferment of gratification, and an understanding that the workplace was more sacred than your home.

Is it just me, or does this sound like a training manual for economic slaves?

Obey. Be on time. Forget happiness. Work is the most important thing in your life.

This is where a thousand years of enlightenment came tumbling down. A thousand years of understanding that there were much more important things to do with your life than work. That would all end, at the hands of religious and political institutions with their own agenda.

Work became salvation, and leisure became evil.

From a Marxist view, what happened was the development of a new industrial system, where workers would accept long hours and low pay, because their religion encouraged them to do so. And that's exactly what happened. People just started to believe work was divine, and their religious influences helped to fuel that fire.

The Rebels: American Settlers

Around this time in world history, a bunch of adventurers were exploring our planet in search of new lands. Why? There were many reasons, but when you look at the earliest settlers in America, they were seeking Aristotle's Eden. The original idea that you would work for leisure, and be free to do what you wanted to do. They wanted to find a new land, with freedom, and the ability to rewrite the rules of working and living.

This happened because not everybody bought into the new idea of the "Protestant work ethic." There were people who knew that something felt fishy in all of that very unnatural religious pressure. Something felt completely wrong with that Protestant work ethic, compared to what they really wanted for their own lives.

Perhaps they were holdovers from the influence of the enlightened Greeks of old. Either way, these initial settlers were willing to risk their lives, crossing the sea to come to a new land with new freedoms.

How ironic it is, that America was settled by people rejecting the religion-driven work ethic. People who were seeking a more fulfilled life.

I wonder what they'd say if they could return today, to see America's culture of working 60 hours a week, sacrificing all elements of life for the prioritization of work. What about our founding fathers' belief that "we hold these truths to be self-evident, that all men are created equal, that they are endowed by their Creator with certain unalienable Rights, that among these are Life, Liberty and the pursuit of Happiness"?

They'd be disgusted. Defining ourselves by our work is not why America was founded. We were founded as a country with ideals far beyond that myopic viewpoint. "How did this happen?" a settler might ask. And to answer that question, we'd look at the carryover of religious influence into the early American culture of work. But beyond that, we'd look at a period of time that would change our work culture for the better.

And then for the worse.

Chapter Two

THE INDUSTRIAL AGE

FORD MOTOR COMPANY WAS QUITE BUSY IN 1908, BUILDING A
magical new type of carriage that required no horses to operate.
These motorized cars would eventually change our world, of
course. But in 1908, Henry Ford had a bit of a problem.

At this time, the average American worker earned between
$200 and $400 per year, and Ford's flagship Model T car was $825.
Labor costs had a huge impact on the price, and in 1908, it was
taking an entire factory of workers to build each car. Together,
they could build a car in 12.5 hours.

These cars were too expensive for the average American,
and production costs were too high to bring the price lower.
He needed a way to build them more quickly and more inexpensively, if he was to make these cars affordable to the masses.

Henry Ford is often credited with what would happen next,
but the truth is that it was already happening in Chicago slaugh-
terhouses and even other automobile manufacturing plants. The
assembly line wasn't Ford's invention. But as with many great
innovators, he was an early mover who brought this technology

to a new level.

After years of experimentation and testing, it was finally ready. On December 1, 1913, Ford's custom-built assembly line began its first day of operation. And the industrial revolution got its rocket ship.

On Ford's new assembly line, cars were now coming out faster than 12.5 hours. *Much* faster. Faster than 10 hours. Faster than 5 hours. We're not talking about a small gain, here. We're talking a complete game-changer.

With the new technologies, Ford began finishing each car in *1 hour and 33 minutes*. In the time it once took to make one car, Ford could now finish *eight* cars. And this entire process required *less* manpower, not more. This was nothing short of a miracle, and it was one of the fastest gains in productivity that the world had ever seen.

With the advent of the assembly lines, Henry Ford was now holding a very different set of cards in this poker game. Now, he had more productivity, more profits, less need for human labor to assemble cars, and more need for specialized human labor to run the new machines.

Old Problems, New Possibilities

At this time in America, the difficult working conditions and low pay for factory workers resulted in two very predictable problems: employee absenteeism and turnover. These were two of the worst kinds of productivity-killers, and they still are.

Think of all the delays involved when a person quits a company: you have to look for a new person, then interview, hire, train, and manage that new person. You have to cover the former employee's work in the meantime, affecting other processes. It's exponentially costly to a business, which is why retaining good employees remains one of the most important and challenging obstacles in business today.

It's safe to say that Ford was constantly thinking of how he could retain his best workers, and attract more of them. So when the assembly line gave him a new set of circumstances and possibilities, he seized the opportunity to solve his labor problems, and create a better deal for everyone.

Henry Ford changed the American workday as we know it, and later explained it all to a journalist named Samuel Crowther. The interview was published 12 years after Ford had initially announced his controversial new innovation: Ford Motor Company would be reducing the length of their workday to an eight-hour day, while simultaneously paying higher wages per day.

Just before this article was published, Ford took this eight-hour workday concept further, reducing the definition of a workweek to five days from the previous standard of six days, while still maintaining the same weekly wages.

The five-day, 40-hour workweek began here, and this interview explains much of Ford's reasoning for it. I find the interview to be a fascinating, beautiful dance. In his carefully-planned words, you can see Ford tiptoeing around the religious assumptions of the time, and the heavily-engrained "Protestant work ethic" that had run rampant in America, extending the workday to excessive hours that consumed the workers' entire lives.

At this time in America, factory workers were working six days a week, and laboring for 10 to 16 hours per day. It was physically exhausting, and it was deadly.

In his 1910 book *Injured in the Course of Work*, writer William Hard estimated that one in five steel workers in Chicago were dying or being severely injured on an annual basis. There were 536,165 workers being killed or maimed in their jobs *every year*, according to the American Institute of Social Service. The population of our country was only about 92 million at the time, so this was over half of one percent of the population!

It's hard to believe it, but this was just normal at the time. It was socially accepted, or at least more so than it would be today. In this interview, Ford needed to find a way to explain all the reasons the excessively long workday is inefficient and terrible, without offending the status quo of the very nation he wanted to sell his cars to.

To accomplish this, Ford acknowledged the then-current religious beliefs, and then he politely stepped past religion and into economics and operations. It's truly amazing, how he navigated this touchy subject.

Here's the 1926 interview with Ford, published in the popular magazine *World's Work*. I've included a few of my insights and explanations along the way.

HENRY FORD: Why I Favor Five Days' Work With Six Days' Pay

The automobile manufacturer in this authorized interview tells Mr. Crowther why he reduced the working week in Ford plants all over the world to forty hours with no cut in pay
By Samuel Crowther

Just twelve years ago, Henry Ford made an announcement which, for the moment, turned industry upside down and brought workmen by the tens of thousands storming for jobs. His announcement was that thereafter the minimum wage in his industries would be five dollars for a day of eight hours. At that time a good wage was two dollars and a half for a day of ten hours. Now he makes another announcement far more important than the one which then went round the world.

"We have," he said, "decided upon and at once put into effect through all the branches of our industries the five day week. Hereafter there will be no more work with us on Saturdays and Sundays. These will be free days, but the men, according to merit, will receive the same pay equivalent as for a full six day week. A day will continue to be eight hours, with no overtime.

"For the present this will not apply to the railroad, and of course it cannot apply to watchmen or the men on certain jobs where the processes must be continuous. Some of these men will have to work Saturdays and Sundays, but they constitute less than one per cent of our working force, and each of them will have two consecutive days off some time during the week. In short, we have changed our calendar and now count a week as five days or forty hours.

"The actual work week of the factories as distinguished from the work week of the men will also be cut to five days. For of course an eight hour man day is not the same as an eight hour factory day. In order to make the full use of our plants we shall as before work the men in shifts.

At this point, Ford has explained that they'll be operating in three separate shifts, eight hours for each shift, in order to achieve the maximum output in the factory. Next, he starts to explain why, and introduce the role of technology in the newly shortened workday.

"We found long ago, however, that it does not pay to put men at work, excepting in continuous operations, from midnight until morning. As a part of low cost production—and only low cost production can pay high wages—one must have a big investment in machinery and power plants. Expensive tools cannot remain idle. They ought to work twenty-four hours a day, but here the human element comes in, for although many men like to work all night and have part of their day free, they **do not work so well and hence it is not economical**, or at least that is our experience, to go through the full twenty-four hours. But a modern factory has to work more than eight hours a day. It cannot be idle two thirds of the time, else it will be costly.

Ford is saying this: these new machines have made humans massively more efficient. Before the machines, humans did all of the work, but humans "do not work so well" in long shifts. He'd found that the most productive combination is this: machines running 24 hours a day, and humans running those machines for eight hours per shift.

Today, we've had a similar effect, where we have new technologies that are able to run 24 hours a day, accomplishing many tasks better than humans can. Our company website at Tower is a great example: it's constantly running, generating leads and closing sales. It runs much more productively than a retail store. But it takes a very sharp, efficient human being to manage that technology at its most productive level.

Therefore, just like Henry Ford was explaining in 1926, we're now in the business of optimizing human energy. To explain that a bit further, Ford's next words begin to move beyond theory. He explains how they're already working a shorter workday, and how it has proven to be more productive.

"This decision to put into effect the short work week is not sudden. We have been going toward it for three or four years. We have been feeling our way. We have during much of this time operated on a five day basis. But we have paid only for five days and not for six. And whenever a department was especially rushed it went back to six days—to forty-eight hours. Now we know from our experience in changing from six to five days and back again that **we can get at least as great production in five days as we can in six, and we shall probably get a greater, for the pressure will bring better methods.** A full week's wage for a short week's work will pay."

Ford's powerful statement—*the pressure will bring better methods*—is one that we will certainly be revisiting in the following pages. That concept is crucial to understand, and believe, in order to have faith in future innovation.

This concept remains true in the world of entrepreneurship and business. Constraining money or time is a surefire way to foster creativity and find solutions to productivity. The pressure of these constraints produce better methods, and that's exactly what Ford found.

Ford's statement was important in establishing the logic of the shorter workday, from a business perspective. If a shorter workday generates higher productivity, then it makes business sense to implement a shorter workday. You'd be crazy to not do this, right?

Next, Ford talks about wages, and why they should be raised, not lowered.

"Does this mean," I asked, "that your present minimum wage of six dollars a day will become a fraction over seven dollars a day that is, the minimum for five days' work will still be thirty-six dollars, just as it was for six days?"

"We are now working out the wage schedules," answered Mr. Ford. "We have stopped thinking in terms of a minimum wage. That belongs to yesterday, before we quite knew what paying high wages meant. Now so few people get the minimum wage that we do not bother about it at all. We try to pay a man what he is worth and we are not inclined to keep a man who is not worth more than the minimum wage.

"The country is ready for the five day week. It is bound to come through all industry. In adopting it ourselves, **we are putting it into effect in about fifty industries**, for we are coal miners, iron miners, lumbermen, and so on. The short week is bound to come, because without it the country will not be able to absorb its production and stay prosperous.

This wasn't a short-term experiment, and that gives his idea more merit. Ford had experimented with this for *three or four years*.

This wasn't a small experiment, either. Ford had extensions into about fifty industries, and they were massive ones. We're talking about tens of thousands—if not hundreds of thousands—of workers. Ford had large corporations and the resources available to spot the efficiencies of the shorter workday and workweek.

Next, Ford begins to explain how this will contribute to our economy, when workers are paid more and have time to spend their money.

"The harder we crowd business for time, the more efficient it becomes. The more well-paid leisure workmen get, the greater become their wants. These wants soon become needs. Well-managed business pays high wages and sells at low prices. Its workmen have the leisure to enjoy life and the wherewithal with which to finance that enjoyment.

"The industry of this country could not long exist if factories generally went back to the ten hour day, because the people would not have the time to consume the goods produced. For instance, a workman would have little use for an automobile if he had to be in the shops from dawn until dusk. And that would react in countless directions, for the automobile, by enabling people to get about quickly and easily, gives them a chance to find out what is going on in the world-which leads them to a larger life that requires more food, more and better goods, more books, more music—more of everything. The benefits of travel are not confined to those who can take an expensive foreign trip. There is more to learn in this country than there is abroad.

"Just as the eight hour day opened our way to prosperity, so the five day week will open our way to a still greater prosperity.

"Of course, there is a humanitarian side to the shorter day and the shorter week, but dwelling on that side is likely to get one into trouble, for then leisure may be put before work instead of after work—where it belongs.

See what Ford did there? He acknowledged the heavily-engrained "Protestant work ethic" and comforted the readers that he wasn't going to debate that work was still number one. Work is still more important than leisure, he assured the devout traditionalists, implying that they wouldn't have to give up their sacred value system.

Then he begins to explain why it's time for a change.

"Twenty years ago, introducing the eight hour day generally would have made for poverty and not for wealth. Five years ago, introducing the five day week would have had the same result. The hours of labor are regulated by the organization of work and by nothing else. It is the rise of the great corporation with its ability to use power, to use accurately designed machinery, and generally to lessen the wastes in time, material, and human energy that made it possible to bring in the eight hour day. Then, also, there is the saving through accurate workmanship. Unless parts are made accurately, the benefits of quantity production will be lost-for the parts will not fit together and the economy of making will be lost in the assembling. Further progress along the same lines has made it possible to bring in the five day week. The progression has been a natural one.

"The eight hour day law to-day only confirms what industry had already discovered, If it were otherwise, then the law would make for poverty instead of for wealth. A man cannot be paid a wage in excess of his production. In the old days, before we had management and power, a man had to work through a long day in order to get a bare living. Now the long day would retard both production and consumption. At the present time the fixing by law of a five day week would be unwise, because industry is not ready for it, **but a great part of industry is ready**, and within a comparatively short time I believe the practice will be so general in industry that it be made universal.

Ford was saying that an eight-hour workday might not work for every type of business yet, but that it will work for many businesses now, and will work for all of industry in the future. That's exactly where I feel we're at today, with the five-hour workday.

Next, Ford begins to deconstruct the traditional belief that giving workers leisure time was costly to the business ("lost time"), and dangerous for the worker (the "idle hands become evil" fear). He also hints at a problem that has resurfaced in today's world: the class privilege of leisure and time, and the selfishness of not sharing this better life with our fellow man.

"It is high time to rid ourselves of the notion that leisure for workmen is either 'lost time' or a class privilege.

"Nature fixed the first limits of labor, need the next, man's inhumanity to man had something to do with it for a long time, but now we may say that economic law will finish the job.

"Old-fashioned employers used to object to the number of holidays in this country. They said that people only abused leisure and would be better off without so much of it.

"Only lately a French professor accounted for the increased consumption of alcohol by pointing to the eight hour day, which he denounced as a device which gives workingmen more time to drink.

"It will be generally granted that if men are to drink their families into poverty and themselves into degeneracy, the less spare time they have to devote to it the better. But this does not hold for the United States. We are ready for leisure. The prohibition law, through the greater part of the country, has made it possible for men and their families really to enjoy leisure. A day off is no longer a day drunk. And also a day off is not something so rare that it has to be celebrated.

"This is not to say that leisure may not be dangerous. Everything that is good is also dangerous—when mishandled. When we put our five dollar minimum wage for an eight hour day into effect some years ago, we had to watch many of our men to see what use they made of their spare time and money. We found a few men taking on extra jobs—some worked the day shift with us and the night shift in another factory. Some of the men drank their extra pay. Others banked the surplus money and went on-living just as they had lived before. But in a few years all adjusted themselves and we withdrew most of our supervision as unnecessary.

Ford had an odd side to him, kind of a dark side, where he was observing what his workers were doing with their personal lives, in their own homes. But this enabled him to speak to the fear of alcohol abuse that was common at that time. Prohibition supporters believed that alcohol was responsible to many of society's problems, and Ford wanted to address that fear and put it to rest.

"It is not necessary to bring in sentiment at all in this whole question of leisure for workers. Sentiment has no place in industry. In the olden days those who thought that leisure was harmful usually had an interest in the products of industry. The mill-owner seldom saw the benefit of leisure time for his employees, unless he could work up his emotions. Now we can look at leisure as a cold business fact.

"It is not easy so to look at leisure, for age-old custom viewed leisure as 'lost time'—time taken out of production. It was a suspension of the proper business of the world. The thought about leisure usually went no further than that here were hard-driven working people who should have a little surcease from their labors.

The motive was purely humane. There was nothing practical about it. The leisure was a loss—which a good employer might take from his profits.

"That the Devil finds work for idle hands to do is probably true. But there is a profound difference between leisure and idleness. We must not confound leisure with shiftlessness. Our people are perfectly capable of using to good advantage the time that they have off—after work. That has already been demonstrated to us by our experiments during the last several years. We find that the men come back after a two day holiday so fresh and keen that they are able to put their minds as well as their hands into their work.

"Perhaps they do not use their spare time to the best advantage. That is not for us to say, provided their work is better than it was when they did not have spare time. We are not of those who claim to be able to tell people how to use their time out of the shops. We have faith that the average man will find his own best way—even though that way may not exactly fit with the programs of the social reformers. We do know that many of the men have been building houses for themselves, and to meet their demand for good and cheap lumber we have established a lumber yard where they can buy wood from our own forests. The men help each other out in this building and thus are meeting for themselves one of the problems in the high cost of living.

"We think that, given the chance, people will become more and more expert in the effective use of leisure. And we are giving the chance.

"But it is the influence of leisure on consumption which makes the short day and, the short week so necessary. The people who consume the bulk of goods are the people who make them. That is a fact we must never forget—that is the secret of our prosperity.

"The economic value of leisure has not found its way into the thought of industrial leaders to any great extent. While the old idea of 'lost time' has departed, and it is no longer believed that the reduction of the labor day from twelve hours to eight hours has decreased production, still the positive industrial value—the dollars and cents value—of leisure, is not understood.

"The hours of the labor day were increased in Germany under the delusion that thus the production might be increased. It is quite possibly being decreased. **With the decrease of the length of the working day in the United States an increase of production has come,** because better methods of disposing of men's time have been accompanied by better methods of disposing of their energy. And thus one good thing has brought on another.

"These angles are quite familiar. There is another angle, however, which we must largely reckon with—the positive industrial value of leisure, because it increases consumption.

"Where people work longest and with least leisure, they buy the fewest goods. No towns were so poor as those of England where the people, from children up, worked fifteen and sixteen hours a day. They were poor because these overworked people soon wore out—they became less and less valuable as workers. Therefore, they earned less and less and could buy less and less.

"Business is the exchange of goods. Goods are bought only as they meet needs. Needs are filled only as they are felt. They make themselves felt largely in leisure hours. The man who worked fifteen and sixteen hours a day desired only a comer to be in and a hunk of food. He had no time to cultivate new needs. No industry could ever be built up by filling his needs, because he had none but the most primitive.

"Think how restricted business is in those lands where both men and women still work all day long! They have no time to let the needs of their lives be felt. They have no leisure to buy. They do not expand.

"When, in American industry, women were released from the necessity of factory work and became the buyers for the family, business began to expand. The American wife, as household purchasing agent, has both leisure and money, and the first has been just as important as the second in the development of American business.

"The five day week simply carries this thought farther.

"The people with a five day week will consume more goods than the people with a six day week. People who have more leisure must have more clothes. They must have a greater variety of food. They must have more transportation facilities. They naturally must have more service of various kinds.

"This increased consumption will require greater production than we now have. Instead of business being slowed up because the people are 'off work,' it will be speeded up, because the people consume more in their leisure than in their working time. This will lead to more work. And this to more profits. And this to more wages. The result of more leisure will be the exact opposite of what most people might suppose it to be.

So at this point, Ford has made a convincing argument about how a shorter workday will spur spending and economic growth for the country. It's safe to say he was right, and so much so that I believe our country currently has the opposite problem: we spend too much money on the wrong things, and rampant consumerism and materialism is eroding our happiness. But in 1926, Americans were not consuming as much as their new technologies were creating, which was an economic problem.

Ford finishes by explaining that this is a new era, with new possibilities, and it's time for change. His final sentence is such an accurate prediction of the future, that it sends a chill through my spine.

"Management must keep pace with this new demand—and it will. **It is the intersection of power and machinery in the hands of management which has made the shorter day and the shorter**

week possible. That is a fact which it is well not to forget.

"Naturally, services cannot go on the five day basis. Some must be continuous and others are not yet so organized that they can arrange for five days a week. But if the task is set of getting more done in five days than we now do in six, then management will find the way.

"The five day week is not the ultimate, and neither is the eight hour day. It is enough to manage what we are equipped to manage and to let the future take care of itself. It will anyway. That is its habit. **But probably the next move will be in the direction of shortening the day rather than the week."**

And there you have it: Henry Ford predicted the five-hour workday. A century ago.

When Ford's entire business changed overnight, with the addition of the machines that created an assembly line, it opened his eyes to what the future might hold. If his business could change so drastically, and so quickly, then it makes sense that he would apply similar changes to his vision of our future.

I bet he thought we wouldn't be working at all, 100 years later. But that would've been a scary thing for workers to hear (as it still seems to be today), so that might be why he stopped short of making any stronger prediction than "shortening the day." He'd already pushed the needle enough, for 1926.

More About Ford's True Intents

There was certainly some humanitarian element to Ford's push for the shorter workday and the shorter workweek, but his primary intent (in my opinion) was money and productivity. He's looking at humans more as machines, trying to make those machines run more efficiently. He was an industrialist, and acknowledged the Protestant work ethic, and prioritization of work over leisure.

That's the major difference between Ford's intent, and mine. Reducing the workday further, to the five-hour workday that is currently working well for us, is about enjoying your life. We're equally focused on the humanitarian side of it, as much as we're focused on the productivity gains. Why? Because our society needs the humanitarian side now, in order for us to increase our individual and collective quality of living.

Ford spoke about how countries became poor, because they couldn't consume goods and kickstart their economy. But today in America, we are not poor in spending. We're exceptionally good at buying things, actually, and getting ourselves into debt to buy even more things. We're not deficient in spending money, in this era.

Instead, we're deficient in our quality of life. We've become too focused on the money and possessions, and not our true quality of life. So we've become a poor country, in terms of education, childhood happiness, family time, and more. We've become less happy, more stressed out. We're increasingly over-weight, unhealthy, and addicted to harmful things.

I believe that giving people more free time would help to address and fix these issues. If you were done with work by 1:00 p.m. every day, it's easy to see how you, depending on your interests, could become a different type of productive. Productive in exercise, learning, parenting, social causes, community, and more. Productivity that advances society, and creates a better world for those around you, goes far beyond merely being productive at your job. Productivity comes in many forms, and all of it can increase our individual and collective quality of life.

But if workplace productivity is what you want to focus on, that's an option. Ford's findings about the productivity gains of a shorter workday are exactly what we've found as well: the pressure will bring better methods. So if that's the purpose that ultimately helps you (or your employer) take the leap of faith into the five-hour workday, then workplace productivity gains can be your "why," even if it's only one part of a larger whole of my reason for writing this book.

Why Not Three Long Days, Instead of Five Shorter Days?

Ford had the resources and time to experiment with the different types of workday lengths, and workweek lengths, so he did. He played around with going from ten hour days to eight-hour days. He also experimented with going to even fewer workdays.

The best results were a combination of the two, the five-day, 40-hour workweek. And to me, it makes complete sense that workers would be more productive by working fewer hours for five days, than for excessive hours in two or three days.

Imagine what happens at your job, if you work 14 hours a day for three straight days. Your work consumes your life for three days, you'll need your first day off to recover, and you are not practicing your trade for four days at a time (most of the week). It's not a healthy balance of your energy. It's just a parade of alternating excesses.

Duolingo, one of the most popular and effective apps in the world for learning a new language, sends a users a daily reminder that it's more effective to practice language learning daily, even if only for a small amount of time.

If you want to become excellent at playing a musical instrument, which is better: 7 hours of practice once a week, or 1 hour a day, everyday?

The cavemen did this. Entrepreneurs are doing this. There's a reason that what humans originally did, is the same thing as what today's most innovative humans are doing: because it's natural and it works. The naturally productive amount of time to work has always seemed to be about three hours a day, seven days a week.

This balances energy, builds consistency, and is a faster path toward mastery of your work. That's what drives productivity, and that's why Ford's experiments led to fewer hours across more days.

Because of this, I don't believe working fewer days is the right innovation, for today's knowledge workers. It's a close second-place finisher, but it doesn't offer the same combination of quality of life and workplace productivity as shorter workdays do.

Another Reason Against Fewer Days: Variability in Communications

The lean manufacturing processes of Toyota are a more recent breakthrough in our modern era, when it comes to driving higher levels of productivity. One major component of lean manufacturing is the elimination of something called variability.

Variability is bad. Variability causes delays in operations, due to needing a unique piece that (often) requires human intervention to solve. In the digital world that many of us are now working within, this variability isn't on an assembly line. It's in our email inboxes and our voicemail.

Our workforce is now globally connected. Most of us are now, or soon will be, intertwined with teammates around our country and around the world. In order to move our projects forward to completion, people in different locations need to work together to push all of these little pieces along, and those little pieces are driven by email and other digital communications.

When an email sits unanswered for three hours, that lengthens the project timeline a little bit. But if that email sits unanswered for three days, that lengthens the project by *a lot.*

This is a huge part of why many of the most successful entrepreneurs I know often work a little bit, every day. Sadly, it's also part of why a lot of (already overworked) 40-hour-work-week employees are checking their email at the dinner table, on the weekends, and during their vacations. They're all trying to eliminate delays in their communication cycle, because that communication cycle is today's version of the assembly line. We need to keep it moving forward.

Becoming a Talent Magnet

I believe Ford's business motivations were his first priority for moving to the eight-hour day, but I also believe he had an altruistic side to him as well, and it impacted the decision he made.

We'd definitely see this as a bit creepy today, but he cared enough about his employees to visit their houses and see how they were spending their new leisure time. If you wanted to work for Ford, you had to commit to certain ways of living to earn your higher-than-normal wage. Those ways of living were, to me, the parts of life that Ford felt were a better way of living.

It could be argued that this was still purely for business purposes, but I give Henry the benefit of the doubt on this one. Regardless of the truth behind Ford's motivation, one thing is for certain: everyone wanted to work for Ford, in 1914.

The same day he announced the reduced workday and workweek, he also announced that he was doubling wages. That was January 5, 1914. By the end of that month, the company reported that over 10,000 people had made the pilgrimage to Detroit, in hopes of receiving one of these jobs. They stood in the frigid winter air, in lines outside the factory.

Retention went up, turnover went down. And almost overnight, he had lured the best workers in America away from all of his competitors, and into Ford Motor Company.

Employee turnover was virtually eliminated, and simultaneously, a huge competitive advantage was gained in having the nation's most talented workers. Productivity yielded even more productivity.

The Pressure He Faced (That I'm Facing Too)

In 1914, Ford's competitors were furious, and up in arms. They told him that he was going to ruin the entire industry, and acted as if his shortened workday was horrible.

I'm getting the same types of comments today, when I talk about moving to a five-hour workday. I've been told not to write this book, or push the idea any further, because of a fear that workers will want it. There's a fear here, among business owners.

I'm more fearful of what happens to our society, if we *don't* do this.

In the days of Ford, it makes sense that many business owners would've felt like Ford was giving away a secret. The assembly lines were making workers ten times more productive, but instead of giving it to the workers, most business owners just wanted to put that money in their own pocket.

But Ford blew the doors wide open, and his competitors had to face that new reality. His competitors at the time were (in my opinion) robber barons, amassing all the wealth from what was effectively a working class of economic slaves who were knowingly being pushed beyond healthy limits.

Sound familiar? It should. It's what's happening right now.

And that's why I believe we can all learn a powerful lesson from what Ford did, and why he did those things. But before we can apply this to our own businesses and society, I want to explain the elements of our current crisis that are a bit different by comparison.

How Today Is Similar, But Different

In the early 1900s, the working class was barely able to meet their needs. If they weren't working, they weren't eating.

Today, that's not the problem, for the most part. Working conditions are much more humane and tolerable now, than they were 100 years ago. Most people have the possessions they need, although many may be blind to it, due to high levels of consumerism and materialism.

The crisis we're in now is less about wages, and more about time. That's a huge difference, and I've already spent time explaining why I believe that many of our society's ills could be fixed if people worked fewer hours per day. There would be more family time, community engagement, sleep, nutrition, exercise, and all the higher pursuits and experiences that drive health and happiness.

Ford needed to help drive more consumerism, but now we need less consumerism, in my opinion. Ford needed his workers to have more money to afford more stuff, and more time to buy that stuff. Today, we have enough stuff, and recent research shows that it's not our possessions that drive our happiness. It's our experiences. And to have experiences, you need free time. We need to give people time to have the experiences that lead to the true enjoyment of life. More free time to do with as we like is the key, not more money.

That's the primary difference I see between 1914 and today, when it comes to why we all need to spend less time at work.

It's Not About Whether It's Possible, It's About Why You Should

What's very similar now to this exact point in 1914, in a way that is downright eerie, is how there have been huge gains in productivity, and it's all being sent straight to the top of the chain. We are at a point in human history where productivity gains make it possible to share both financial gains and time gains with workers, but thus far, most businesses and most owners are not doing it.

I'll spend the next few chapters explaining how you can implement a five-hour workday, and the business reasons that you should try it. But for these next few paragraphs, I'd like to explain the larger ethical reasons that I believe we should be reducing our workdays.

Honestly, I could run Tower Paddle Boards with four people. I could generate $10 million this next year with four people, and pay them $40,000 each, and keep the rest for myself. Should I do that?

Seriously, I'm asking you: should I do that?

Your answer to that question reveals which ethical system you subscribe to.

If you currently subscribe to our current Wall-Street-driven system of "market ethics," where your only goal is to maximize shareholder value, then you've got no problem with me paying the lowest possible wages, and keeping the profits for myself.

If it's "virtue ethics," however, you might be a little bit uneasy about keeping all those profits. Virtue ethics were the way of life for Aristotle and the ancient Greeks, during a time of great societal progress and enlightenment. This is the ethical system of thinking about not only how an action benefits you personally, but how it benefits the group, and also what your underlying intentions are.

By nature, we are all selfishly oriented. It's how we survive. But any entrepreneur knows that it's not the best way to do business, and it's not the best way to go far in this world. Aside from generally being a decent person who wants to share where possible, lift others up where possible, and help the larger society around me, I want to build great businesses and do great things in this world.

In my experience I've found that the more you give, the more you get. The super successful people that I've encountered almost always offer to help me and others first before asking for favors, and often never ask for any favors. Ask nothing, and unselfishly give everything you can.

I've tried to mimic this, and it simply works. This has taught me that if we can fight our selfish nature, we'll actually do much better and go much farther. I have little interest in hoarding my way to the top of the profit maximization game, but even if I did, I know it's not the fastest or most assured strategy.

I believe that the better thing for all of us to do with this new opportunity, and this new level of productivity, is to share the wealth. Share it in wages, share it in more time off, share it in creating more jobs. Many companies say they do this, but few of them do. Wages are stagnant, benefits are worse, hours are excessive.

I believe it's better to share this wealth and create more jobs, because at the end of the day, we need to live in our society. There's a reason that societies with huge income disparities aren't safe, and this is where it starts. Greed and lack of empathy.

If you've held down the lower and middle classes, and workers feel no ability to improve their lot in life, then it's going to end in revolt. And shouldn't it? Shouldn't we all feel like we have a chance to improve our lives, and have fruitful work? Shouldn't we all retain our unalienable rights to life, liberty, and the pursuit of happiness?

If we feel no chance to improve our lives, we'll have excessive drug addiction, depression, violence, and all of the things that are starting to happen with alarming frequency now. I believe these symptoms of unhappiness will go away, if we bring everybody up in the same way that a rising tide lifts all boats.

In America, we're at an important decision point. And that decision needs to come from America's small and mid-sized business owners, who create the majority of American jobs.

Do we want our country to look more like Denmark and Sweden, where crime is almost non-existent and citizens are the happiest in the world?

Or do we want our country to have a servant class, with violent revolts toward the gated communities where the rich stockpile their resources (but the rich can't walk safely down a public street)?

We're at the point where we need to decide whether we want to have a happy and healthy society, or one where kidnappings and violence and revolt is commonplace. I know which society I want to live in.

Giving employees more of their time back (with the same or better wages) is the best way I know how to make my contribution toward that type of society. A society where success is *shared.*

Henry Ford made his announcement in 1914, proved it was possible and profitable, and encouraged all business owners to see the benefits of the 40-hour workweek. And yet, it wasn't officially implemented as America's standard until 1938, a full *24 years later.*

Ford was early with the eight-hour workday in 1914, and very similarly, I know that my company is early with the five-hour workday. But we're not 24 years early. Enough companies are interested and experimenting with this, that the shorter workday will be here soon. And just like Ford experienced, and like I'm experiencing now at Tower, your company will enjoy a powerful advantage if you begin before your competitors do.

And trust me when I say this: it will transform your culture, and the lives of everyone in it, for the better.

Chapter Three

THE INFORMATION AGE

——

THE INFORMATION AGE IS NOW UPON US, AND HISTORY IS repeating itself. But this time, it's a bit different.

In a recent movie about Steve Jobs, there's a very pointed moment when Jobs (played by Ashton Kutcher) says that computers are tools created for the mind. To me, that's essentially what's happened during the information age: we've created productivity tools for the mind.

When people are asked to define the history of "hard work," it's natural to think of physical labor. Cutting rocks, lifting them, carrying them into place. It's intuitive and natural to understand that after 12 hours a day of doing this hard work, a person would be exhausted, and their productivity would go down with each additional hour of work.

This is the problem that was solved in the industrial age. Machines were invented to move these rocks, and do all of the physically-intensive work faster than humans. Humans could now do their jobs much faster, and the productivity gains made it possible to reduce the number of working hours, without sacrificing profitability.

The productivity gains of the industrial age are easier to understand. It makes sense to all of us, why machines could help us reduce the long factory hours to an eight-hour workday. But when the conversation transitions into today's productivity issues (and specifically in the world of knowledge workers and computer-based work), it's harder for most people to identify and understand.

In this era, the machines now do most of the physical work. Now, we do the work that only our minds can do. We're exercising our minds now, much more than our bodies. In fact, many of us are sitting at office desks so long that the sustained immobility is actually creating health issues. This exercising of the mind is very taxing on both your body and your mind.

That's why we still get tired and need to sleep at night. It's to regenerate your body, but it's also to regenerate and reset your mind. Our minds must be sharper now, and rested, in order for us to not go crazy.

In the information age, we've created tools for the mind, because that's what we needed next. The industrial age gave us the tools to do the work of our bodies, but now we need tools to further leverage our minds.

Thanks to innovators like Gates, Jobs, Zuckerberg, Page, Brin, and thousands of other contributors to the technologies of the information age, many of those tools have been created. As a result, our minds have been given the same gift as our bodies received 100 years ago: we're able to accomplish our work in a much shorter period of time. In fact, we're able to accomplish work now that was not even possible before.

But unlike last time, these productivity gains weren't passed on to the workers. Not yet, anyway. Instead, we're simply working more hours. We're using our higher levels of productivity to (attempt) to accomplish more work. But that just doesn't work, because our minds don't work the same way our bodies do.

What's happening now is that we're overworking the mind.

We've got unprecedented amounts of stress, mental illness, and breakdowns that manifest as physical illnesses. An eight-hour workday, for a knowledge worker, is like a 16-hour day for the industrial laborer. It's pushing the majority of humans past their limits, and with the productivity gains of today and tomorrow, it's no longer the best business decision to keep doing this.

It's Happening At Your Company Already, If You Look For It

What's really happening today is this: knowledge workers are accomplishing two to three good hours of work in a day. They might be stretching it across an eight-hour day, but the truth is, they're likely only accomplishing two to three hours of solid, productive work.

Why? Because they can. Because we've now got these technologies that have enabled our minds to become massively more productive, and this trend will only continue. Many of your most talented employees and co-workers already know this, but they have no incentive to admit it. Our current workweek trains people to spread out their work to fill their workdays, and rewards them for doing it.

Because we've had a huge increase of productivity, and it's happened so quickly, it's also possible that people are just working inefficiently. They're not realizing their work could've been finished in three hours, instead of eight. But again, what incentive do they have to think this way, and innovate?

If a worker's job is to move 10 items and they have eight hours to do it, and a new machine now enables them to move more items than before, what do you think typical worker will do? Obviously you need a little more information to solve this problem.

Let's say you think that this machine will make the worker twice as fast (you don't know because it's new), so you ask the worker to double their work to 20 items. The worker, upon beginning to do the work, quickly realizes that it's possible to move 100 items a day. That's how technology today is, it's better than people realize, and it keeps getting better every year.

But this worker, knowing he's got to stay at work for at least eight hours, has no incentive to move more than 20. In fact, if he moves more than 20, then he's got no room for "improvement" when performance reviews come around.

The worker has every incentive to move exactly 20 items. Is it any surprise to us then, when he only moves 20 a day?

This is exactly what's happening now, in the information age. You've already got these efficiencies and gains in productivity, whether you know it or not. There's just no incentive for workers to find or utilize that productivity, in most companies.

That's why I believe most people are just stretching out three hours' worth of work across their 8-10 hour workday. I'm not saying the people are lazy, either. I'm saying they're doing what they're incentivized to do.

The better bargain, for both the employer and the employee, is to incentivize productivity by working faster and getting the hell out of there. Receiving the same pay (or more), with more time to go live your life. That's quite a reward, and people would be incredibly motivated by that.

But instead, we all fill our time at work, because we're paid on a 40 hour workweek.

History Repeats Itself: An 80% Productivity Gain, But No Benefit to Workers (Yet)

History has repeated itself, with a different result.

We have new machinery. We have new automation. Productivity has skyrocketed. But the labor side of the equation didn't change. We haven't reduced workers' hours, or the number of days, or even increased pay much at all on average. It's ridiculous.

In the past 40 years, the average worker has become 80% more productive. For knowledge workers, it's going to be much higher than that. And how much have wages gone up, in that same period?

Eleven percent.

Can you blame the workers, for only doing as much as necessary? Where is their incentive here?

And worse yet, our most talented workers are working *more hours* for the same pay! The average American worker is logging 47 hours per week now. About 25% of our workers report working more than 50 hours a week, and another 25% report working more than *60 hours a week.*

How insane is this? We exponentially more productive than we were 40 years ago, and yet we're working 20-50% more hours per week? And we're doing it for 11% more pay? If you want a recipe for a societal crisis, this seems like a pretty good one.

An adjustment is long overdue.

I believe that this is part of what Tim Ferriss exposed with his book *The Four Hour Workweek.* The book caused an explosive amount of entrepreneurship and innovation in small companies, because the book explains exactly how to leverage these new technologies to accomplish anything more quickly than ever.

By showing people exactly how to do it, Ferriss proved that these gains in productivity are right here for the taking. For all of us.

As a result, thousands of entrepreneurs like me took advantage of these new opportunities, and built companies for ourselves. Talented employees went to the freelance or consulting side, to get out of their wasteful office environments. These two types of workers—entrepreneurs and freelance workers—both have an incentive to pursue this newly-available productivity.

That incentive is *time*. Time to enjoy life.

All of this is happening now, but only in that small little part of our economy: the solo entrepreneurs and the small disruptive upstarts. It hasn't happened in our larger economy yet, for our entire society. And I believe that it should.

It's Not Just Our Working Hours That Need Updating

As a society, it seems like we should be able to look at our institutions and understand why they need updated, when the needs of our society have changed. But we don't do this, and we continue doing things that make no sense to anyone, because it's natural to resist change.

American adults aren't the only ones dealing with outdated traditions on a daily basis. Every summer, our kids prove that they're stuck inside of something quite similar: an outdated, completely senseless nine-month school schedule.

The nine-month school calendar is rooted in the agricultural age. And it made sense then. In 1870, 70-80% of Americans were employed in agriculture. There was so much labor and help needed in the summer that they actually had the children working as well, and so the children couldn't go to school in the summer. Makes perfect sense.

Fast forward to the industrial age, when parents began going to work in factories, and child labor laws were enacted. There was no need for kids to be off all summer, but it wasn't problematic, because many families had the mother home full-time.

Now we're in the information age, and it's beyond absurd. Less than 2% of Americans are employed in agriculture. Most families have both parents working. The summer breaks interrupt a child's learning, and slow down their development (especially children from disadvantaged homes). The cost of childcare for the summer cripples our already struggling middle class and lower class.

There's absolutely no reason for kids to not be in school year-round, with breaks sprinkled in throughout the year. It's just another example of how our society can be so slow to change, despite having all the reasons to make that change.

The 40-hour workweek is the same type of problem. We're all still doing something we've always done, despite the fact that it no longer makes any sense. It's this collective delusion that we must continue to do it, staying at work for eight hours or more per day, to do three hours of work. Driving to work in the dark, coming home in the dark.

All for no good reason.

America's True Workweek, Today

I've already mentioned the statistics surrounding American working hours, but they bear repeating. The 40 hour workweek is what we think our baseline is, but it isn't.

In 2014, Gallup reported the results of its survey of American workers, to reveal how many hours they were actually working per week. Take a look at this chart of the results.

Average Hours Worked by Full-Time U.S. Workers, Aged 18+

Self-reported hours typically worked each week, based on pay structure

	Paid a salary	Paid hourly
	%	%
60+ hours	25	9
50 to 59 hours	25	17
41 to 49 hours	9	12
40 hours	37	56
Less than 40 hours	3	8
Weekly average	**49 hours**	**44 hours**

Based on Gallup's 2014 Work and Education poll, conducted Aug. 7-10, 2014

The average full-time American worker averages 47 hours, and the average salaried worker logs 49 hours on average. We all know the reason why salaried workers get the worst end of the spectrum: employers don't have to pay them overtime wages.

Look at the numbers of workers who work 40 hours or less. For hourly workers, who would have to be paid overtime wages for any hours logged over 40 hours, 64% of workers are kept at the 40 hour standard or less. But for salaried workers, it's only 40%. They're grinding more hours, with 50% working 50 hours or more.

One thing is for sure: working hours have gone up. But the problem is, wages haven't. And that's a huge part of the inequality that is becoming quite a problem, when it comes to both money and time to enjoy life.

But believe it or not, there are places where it's worse.

South of The Border: Mexico

A year or two ago, we were looking at building a factory across the border from San Diego, in the country of Mexico. The city of Tijuana is only 30 minutes away, so we were looking at having our paddle boards made there.

I began looking at the factories there, talking to existing factory owners, and they started explaining to me the Mexican workweek. I was beyond shocked. I had no clue that, just across our border, workers had a six-day workweek and worked at least eight hours per day. And that's just their standard, which is probably lower than many people work.

A lot of people in America believe Mexico is a poor country where nobody works much, but that couldn't be more wrong. They're working harder and longer than we are. Seeing this made me wonder what else there was that I didn't know about other countries' working hours.

Let's go to a very different place: France.

France's 35-Hour Week: Fewer Hours, More Jobs

France actually legislated a 35-hour workweek in 2000, and brought their working hours down from their previous level of 40 hours a week. The perception of France's lower working hours is that it's all about work-life balance, and it is about that, to some degree. But what's forgotten is that this was done in France to spur more employment.

France was having an unemployment problem, and they were hoping that limiting each worker's hours would create extra jobs in their economy. If every seven jobs worked five fewer hours, then a new 35-hour job would be created, in theory. The theory appeared to have worked, with unemployment being reduced by 15%.

This is similar to what the United States did in 1938, when they reduced our workweek to 40 hours. That was also an attempt to distribute the total hours across more people, and increase employment.

How America Compares to Other Countries, in Wages and Workweek

In the US, we're working an average 47 hours per week, and making about $50,000 on average. How does this compare?

In a 2013 post on CNNMoney.com, here are the average working hours and earnings in ten other developed countries around the world. Earnings are in US dollars.

- Netherlands: 29 hours, $47,000
- Denmark: 33 hours, $46,000
- Norway: 33 hours, $44,000
- Ireland: 34 hours, $51,000
- Germany: 35 hours, $40,000
- Switzerland: 35 hours, $50,000
- Belgium: 35 hours, $44,000

- Sweden: 36 hour, $38,000
- Australia: 36 hours, $45,000
- Italy: 36 hours, $34,000

All ten of those developed countries are working less than us. If we assume that our workweek is actually 47 hours on average, many of those countries would be earning more than us too, per hour.

The Other Side of The Coin

There are countries that have it much worse than we do, however. If you look at India, they work six days a week, ten hours a day. They're working 60 hour weeks as a norm, whereas only 25% of Americans are working those hours.

I already talked about Mexico, and China is the absolute extreme. The posted hours are eight hours a day, six days a week, but that's not even close to what they work. They're working 12 hour days, six days a week. It's insane. Their entire life is devoted to work, and they're being paid a very small wage.

What's happening in China now is similar to what happened during the industrial revolution in America. There's a working class of 700 million people being exploited, a middle class of about 300 million people being paid livable wages, and a super-rich wealthy class that is enjoying all the productivity gains. It's a huge difference in prosperity.

My Takeaway From This Wide Range of Working Hours, Globally

When I look at the wide range of working hours from country to country, my takeaway is this:

Why are we holding on so tight to this 40-hour workweek, as if it's some kind of standard? There is no standard, and the data proves it. And yet, when I tell people about a five-hour workday, or 25-hour workweek, some people tell me that's insane and impossible.

Oh yeah? Don't tell that to the Netherlands, then. Because they're working 29 hours a week, and earning more than us, per hour. Don't tell Sweden, either, because they're currently headed toward a six-hour workday. A October 2015 CNN article said that Sweden had found the shorter workday to result in "more productivity and higher morale."

Recent Experiments With Shorter Workweeks or Workdays

Because of everything we've discussed so far, I believe it's only a matter of time before it will be normal to have a shorter workday and/or workweek. It's happening already with freelancers and very small companies, and some larger companies across the country and world are now beginning to experiment with it.

One of the largest experiments we've seen so far in America took place in Utah, in 2008. The state was having some budget challenges, and wanted to reduce their energy expenses by 20%, so they reduced their workdays by 20%. In August of 2008, over 17,000 government employees learned that they'd have every Friday off.

The catch, unfortunately, is that they'd still have to work 40 hours a week, as four 10-hour workdays. The short term benefits were that government offices would stay open longer hours (which of course would help the average American worker use those services, since they're working 9.4 hours per day).

In the end, Utah saved 13% on their energy consumption, but some other interesting consequences happened along the way: productivity was reported to be up by 9%, and 70% of workers said they were much happier as a result of the new schedule.

A company named 37Signals built one of the best productivity tools of the modern era, a project management program called Basecamp. This is a very forward-thinking, modern company.

In 2012, they moved to a 32-hour workweek, of four eight-hour days, from May to October.

This is a company that builds productivity tools, so it's no surprise to me that they found more productivity in reducing their working hours. This is better than what Utah did, in my opinion, because 37Signals actually reduced the total working hours, instead of simply shifting them around.

Eliminating a workday and going down to 32 hours per week is one possible path to the same end, or at least the start of it. But as I mentioned earlier, I don't think that reducing the number of days is the way to go, just yet. I think our most productive starting point would be to reduce the hours of the five-day workweek, and it's because we need to rest our minds.

Remember, in the industrial age, we created tools for the body. We reduced the number of days to give the body a break. But reducing days and adding hours to those days—like four 10-hour days—is not what we truly need next. This doesn't address the true crisis, which is a lack of brainpower, daily rest, and overall balance in our lives.

One Employee's Powerful Insight About 10-Hour Days

When NBC reported on Utah's experiment with 10-hour days, they ended their story with a quote from a worker named Debra, and her words really say it all. Not just for the failures of a 10-hour workday, but also for the 9.4 hour workdays that we're all averaging now.

"After working 10 hours in a day," she said, "I don't do anything after I get home."

This is true for nearly all of us, but we have no incentive to admit it. Quite the opposite: most of us are going to do everything we can to support it and ask for it to continue.

Why? Because if you're the average salaried American, you're already effectively working 10 hours a day. You're working 47 hours a week, which is 9 hours and 24 minutes per day. And there's a 50% chance that you're working 10 hours or *more*, five days a week.

For the average American, a four-day workweek of 10-hour days looks like this: a free day off. Because it is. There is every reason in the world to support this, if you're an employee. That's why we don't see more comments like the one Debra made.

The Utah situation presented a rare opportunity for a reporter to ask Debra a question that few employees are asked: what is the *downside* of a 10-hour workday?

If we were all asked this question more often, and if we observed our lives in search of the answer to that question, then we'd understand why Debra's answer is the simple and honest truth.

Debra works in Medicaid services, and that's a knowledge worker job. She's not moving rocks all day, she's using her mind all day. Adding hours to the workday will drive down productivity in either case, but *especially* in knowledge work.

Our brains require a more intense energy than our bodies do. There's no way that most human brains can accomplish truly productive knowledge work for 10 hours a day, or eight hours, or even six hours. That's why Debra is drained when she gets home.

And think about it: when you get home after an abnormally long day, and you're drained, what goes to the wayside? Exercise. Community. Family time. Learning. Other enjoyable experiences and relationships.

Happiness. Happiness goes by the wayside.

Meanwhile, if you're someone who depends on a service that Debra provides, and you don't get what you need by Thursday, then what happens? You don't have it Friday. Or Saturday. Or Sunday. The "assembly line" of services in your life, and in this business, has come to a screeching halt.

I don't know about you, but I don't think that productivity is optimized in an environment of drained employees and stalled processes. You can find the data out there, just like Utah did, that will make this appear to be successful. Already overworked employees have every incentive to say their lives are better with a four-day workweek, and to do what they can to show that they're more productive.

Remember the example of the worker moving rocks, but holding back on his true productivity unlocked by the new machine? Moving 20 rocks instead of 100? Well, this is where that holding back pays off. The worker gets the free day off, moves 30 rocks the next week, and says "I'm 50% more productive now! Thanks boss!"

For the state of Utah in 2008, I don't think a five-hour workday would have been appropriate for the problem they were attacking, or the services they needed to provide to the public. But my point is this: if the same sample size of 17,000 workers had been given a five-hour workday, and asked them to accomplish the same tasks in half the time, Utah would've achieved a *much* higher productivity gain than 9%.

And productivity aside, how would Debra's quote change at the end of that NBC story, if she was working only five hours per day instead of ten? How would her daily life change? How might her entire family's life change?

In this Information Age, we now have a dizzying array of tools, harnessing an increasingly unknown amount of power that help us to leverage our mind. More tools are created every day. Now, we need to rest our minds, so that we can not just run these new machines, but run them to full advantage. There is only one way to do that, in my opinion: work fewer hours per day. The pressure will bring better methods, and it will force us to optimize the use of these new machines.

And most importantly, it will change our lives and society for the better.

PART II

—

INFORMATION AGE WORK AND LIFESTYLE

Chapter Four

HOW WE'RE WORKING TODAY

———

WE'RE SO BUSY WITH OUR LIVES THESE DAYS, THAT IT'S HARD for most people to realize how dramatically things have changed in such a short period of time. I graduated from high school in 1990, and that was also the first year that my family owned a home computer. It was rare to own one, back then. And it was difficult to understand the value of them.

In high school, if I had to write a paper, I'd ask my mom to bring home a typewriter from her office. They had fancy typewriters, with the technology that allowed you to actually backspace and correct an error. This was a huge deal, when you wanted to write a paper. Can you imagine typing an email today, or a document of any kind, knowing that you could not make any errors in typing?

At the bank where my mom worked, she had a telephone on her desk, and it needed a cord to function. She didn't have a computer. But she did have a typewriter, and lots of postage stamps... because *fax machines* weren't even widely used yet. This was only 25 years ago.

These were knowledge workers, in 1990. It's mind-blowing, to think how less productive and efficient their days were, compared to our days now. They needed to have all of their meetings, all of their group discussions, *in person.* Everybody needed to drive or fly to the meeting location, just to even have the type of discussion that (today) we'd have in an email.

From that point on, to understand the massive gains in productivity in the knowledge working world, we've really got to list out exactly what happened next.

How Everything Changed, and Quickly

Word processors came along, and they were a huge advance in technology. It saved an incredible amount of time to be able to change words without needing whiteout, or needing to start over completely.

Then came the first computers, with their ability to do some basic math for you, and store small documents. Then spreadsheets came along, and blew the doors wide open. Spreadsheets had automated calculations, at a time when every calculation was done manually, on paper. Imagine how that changed the lives of accountants, or retailers, or bankers.

Then came cell phones. The first ones were huge bricks that people carried around. But it began to untether people from their offices, and that was huge for many industries right away.

Then came the biggest game-changer of all: the internet. Almost immediately, it changed the way humans had communicated for thousands of years. E-mail replaced letters, and now, it's replaced much more than that. Meetings. Records. File storage. Your entire memory, really. Now you can go just go back and read your e-mails, to remember what people said, or remember where a project stood.

Obviously, the combinations of all these technologies were life-changing, and they freed up our brains to drive even higher levels of productivity. With our brains having new tools, the pace of innovation became even faster.

Consider how we travel now. In 1990, we needed a travel agent. It was expensive, slow, and complicated. Now we book online, and we don't even have to print anything to board our airplanes.

Need a taxi? In 2010, we had to wave one down, or call one and wait for it, and then we had to pay their expensive fares. But now we have Uber. Now there's a personal car service just waiting for everybody, saving us time and money. Game-changing, again.

Want to go on a date? Think of how slow and inefficient that was, before online dating. That's why 35% of all marriages in 2013 were people who said they initially met online, according to a June 2013 article on USNews.com.

Look at how Facebook has changed our lives. Entire books will be written on that alone. In terms of time savings, look at how much easier it is to assemble your friends or family, for any type of event. Happy hours, class reunions, political rallies... you name it. Facebook connected nearly all of us.

There are hundreds of other examples of how technology has changed the way we live. It was happening so fast in the early 2000s that it was hard to even realize how much our lives were changing. Nobody had really tied these capabilities together in a way that explained how to leverage them to accomplish your work faster and improve your life. Nobody until Tim Ferriss, that is.

The Wakeup Call

Tim Ferriss' book, *The Four Hour Workweek*, focused on leveraging these new capabilities to outsource all the things you don't want to do, in order to pursue the life you want. He highlighted lesser-known technologies and websites that had recently become available, sites like oDesk and Elance, where there was access to extremely inexpensive labor all over the world.

The concept started with small tasks to supplement your life, like having a virtual assistant. But then it expanded into everything else that knowledge businesses needed: computer programmers, graphic designers, writers, social media marketers, and anything that could be done online. And not necessarily in a way that would replace your employees' jobs or your own, but instead to leverage time to accomplish tasks of higher value.

That's productivity. That turns each employee into their own business unit, acting like a business owner themselves, managing the efforts of other people around the world.

After reading that book, I think entrepreneurs like me became especially observant of how to leverage our new technologies to accomplish things that were nearly impossible a decade earlier.

Becoming Your Own Media Powerhouse (For Free)

When it comes to a radical transformation of our media and how we consume it, I can think of no better example than YouTube and online video.

A couple of years ago, a fellow entrepreneur Alex and his wife Mimi decided to start a YouTube channel, where Mimi was showing the different ways of doing her hair. It was just the two of them, with basically no expertise to start. Today, they have 2.6 million subscribers on YouTube. Their videos have been viewed over 318 *million* times.

To put this in perspective, the Super Bowl has always been America's most-watched television event of the year. The 2015 Super Bowl was the most-watched Super Bowl ever. How many views did it have?

It had 114 million views. Alex and Mimi have 204 million more video views than the most-watched *Super Bowl.* That's how much the video world has changed. It's another powerful example of something that simply was not possible, until now.

The business they've wrapped around this media powerhouse is called LuxyHair.com. It's profitable, and not just a little bit. Their business clears over *seven figures.* That's how fast a business can grow now in just a few years.

It's no surprise, then, that I fully understand how YouTube can help our own Tower Magazine (http://Tower.Life) become the best beach lifestyle company in the world. We're creating content people love, and getting new subscribers everyday, and learning to take advantage of this new capability.

How Online Discussion Groups Flipped The Sales Funnel

When it comes to market research and product development, the internet has given us something beautiful: discussion groups. Every business can find all the qualitative research they need in online discussion groups.

I learned everything I needed to know about poker chips from poker player discussions online. They'd talk about the sizes, the weights, the colors, who the manufacturers are. Those people knew more about my industry than I did, as an owner. And they not only helped me develop products for free, but in the end, they became my best customers.

You can leverage online discussion groups for much more than research. You can do your product development there, crowdsource ideas, discuss prototypes and features, and ultimately build an online community of fans who want your products before you even *build* them.

Imagine how much time this saves, compared to the old way (the way huge, wasteful corporations are still doing business today). You pay for a boatload of market research, pay in-person focus groups, pay expensive designers, pay a PR department to blast advertising to publications, and pay all the marketing and sales personnel to follow it up.

Instead, my poker chip business was just me—a one-man business replacing all of those traditional functions—by leveraging discussion groups online and building a community there. For *free*.

These online groups are self-selected, by their interests, and you can find the groups that are 100% relevant to your business.

What's really funny is that this is stuff I was using ten years ago! Today, the tools available for this type of product development research, proof of concept, and pre-sales has exploded. Kickstarter can do much of what I was doing before with discussion groups, except a whole lot more efficiently. It's proof of concept and an initial sales tool in a box. And the list of other inexpensive (or even free) tools is long and growing everyday.

Today, what myself and many others refer to as the "Golden Age of Entrepreneurship," is a business owner's dream come true. And yet, I see businesses everywhere wasting time and money, doing things the old, slow, expensive way.

Maybe if they had to accomplish their job in five hours, they'd finally utilize these technologies.

The Sky Is the Limit, Thanks to the Cloud

Another massive productivity-enhancer is DropBox. That technology enables you to put your work online, accessible from any device in your life. This productivity tool alone has untethered people from not just their office, but any particular computer. So for people who travel for work, they're still productive from anywhere, and not bottlenecking any projects or processes while they're gone.

Teleconferencing is another technology that changed communications a decade ago, and Skype took that one step further. Clear and inexpensive teleconferencing, via audio or even video, worldwide. Again, compare it to my mom's bank in 1990. If they'd had teleconferencing and Skype, they would've been able to have more meetings in less time, without needing to leave their office. It probably would've made them 10 times more efficient and productive.

Overnight Experts Everywhere

Training yourself and your staff is now lightning fast, thanks to online learning. Conferences still exist, but they're mainly for networking benefits now, not learning. Colleges still exist, but they're ridiculously expensive and slow to teach the newest information. Online learning is fast, and in many cases, free.

When I hire a new employee and they have the capability of becoming an expert in something we need them to be an expert in, the conversation goes like this:

Me: "Welcome to the team! I want you to become an expert on this topic. You've got three to six months to do that."

New team member: "Wow, okay. Do I have a budget to go to conferences or seminars or local classes?"

Me: "No. It's all online, and free."

And that conversation seems to apply to almost every skill we need in our business.

In 1990, it might have taken you 20 years to become an expert on a new subject. You'd have to go to some expensive, slow university, and take a bunch of classes that were irrelevant. You'd have to get magazines and books and newspapers, and sift through a bunch of information you didn't want, to learn the things you did. But now, with a dedicated effort for 3-6 months, you can become an expert on almost anything in the online marketing world. For *free.*

Education has changed. YouTube has the greatest lecturers in the world, whether they're professors or kid geniuses. You don't need to memorize anything, it's at your fingertips. There are interest groups and online forums of people who help each other learn things, and practice them. You have everything you need to learn it, test it, and master it.

Aiming For 10x

What most people miss when they think about today's pace of technological advancement is how fundamentally life-altering the changes really are. Most people think of technological advancement in terms of going from cassette tapes to CDs. You get a more durable and more portable item, it holds more data, and it reproduces sound at a superior quality. Those are nice upgrades, for sure, but they are really just incremental improvements. The music industry didn't get totally disrupted when this happened.

The technology advances that we are going through today are more akin to the shift from CDs to digitally delivered music, whether it's pirating like Napster or new disruptive pricing and delivery models like with iTunes. This isn't an incremental change. This is a 10x change, or more really, because the music industry is totally and forever disrupted. What used to work will no longer work. People's experience with music totally changes as well.

These types of 10x changes are the lofty aspirations that today's leading technology companies like Google and Tesla aspire to, and are achieving. This is about totally rethinking problems and exploring what's technically possible from a blank slate. They call this reasoning from first principles: asking what we are sure is true at the fundamental level, and then reasoning up from there.

To give you an example of how revolutionary a new knowledge working tool of this nature can be, I will tell you about how I source new products today using Panjiva.com. If you are in the business of making and selling products, what I'm about to tell you is something I typically tell only my best friends, and it's literally worth millions. That should justify the cost of this book.

Panjiva is a website that aggregates Homeland Security data on all shipping containers that come into the US. The date, the weight, a general description of contents, its origination, and its destination is information that has to be on file. It is public information, accessible to anyone. Panjiva simply aggregates it, and makes it searchable. This changes everything.

Prior to Panjiva, I would source new products using something like Alibaba.com, which in itself is an amazing advancement over traditional sourcing of factories and products overseas. Factories list what they make on Alibaba and US companies can search by products and identify factories to manufacture their products.

The problem is that if you search for "paddle boards," there might be 2,000 companies that claim to make them. A handful are good factories, another handful are bad factories, a huge chunk are non-necessary intermediaries, and a bunch are fakes or scammers. Good luck with deciding who you're going to send a $50,000 check to and hope some quality goods (or any goods at all) actually get shipped to you. And this is the modern "good" solution for sourcing that is light years ahead in terms of efficiency, compared to having to get on a plane and make friends and do research in person overseas.

Product development and factory identification used to be a really expensive, time consuming, and risky process. We're talking tens or hundreds of thousands of dollars and years of time to dial things in right. You may have to start with one factory, and move to another. You might get screwed by one and lose $20,000. And you'd spend a lot of time on airplanes and on the ground in various overseas countries. With Alibaba, things got exponentially faster and that's what most people use today and they love it. In fact, its IPO in 2014 was the largest IPO in the history of the world. It's a valuable tool.

Using Panjiva, I can type in a product like "paddle boards" and it will show me all the containers coming into the country that mention paddle boards in the contents. It will show me the date of each, how much it weighed, what factory sent it, and what customer received it. It will show me this data over time, and I can drill down to all the shipments coming from one factory, or alternatively all of the shipments arriving to one customer.

I can search on my competitor's name and find their factories. I can see how many shipments they are getting and if that's growing over the past few years. I can then search on their factory and find the other companies who are supplied by that factory, and whether their shipments are increasing or decreasing over time. Long term relationships and increasing shipments guarantee I've found a reliable factory. I can almost get market share data from this.

This one tool reduces the sourcing process from years of research, and tens or hundreds of thousands of dollars, to an afternoon on the computer. This is 10x stuff. I have no worries cutting a $50,000 check to a factory I find on Panjiva without ever meeting them. In fact, I've been an entrepreneur sourcing and selling products since 2003, and the first time I ever set foot in China was last year, 2015.

You know what the funny thing is? When I tell a business associate about how I use Panjiva, rarely has anyone ever even heard of it. I'm talking about pretty serious business people that run or work at $10M or $100M+ businesses. I've spoken to university classes where a lot of the students take high level classes on procurement. No one knows about this.

You know what else is funny? Panjiva has been around for almost a decade!

For an updated list of more amazing productivity tools like Panjiva, check FiveHourWorkday.com.

And Yet...

All of these technologies I've mentioned have been around for long enough that every business can utilize them. And yet, few are doing that. Why?

There's a resistance to change, and there's no immediate and obvious reason for most businesses to think they need to change. There's no time constraint, because they're in the office for much longer than they need to be, to accomplish their three hours of work.

In 1990, we were really working eight hours a day, because everything from typing a letter to having a meeting was inefficient and slow. Now, we've basically got nuclear firepower at our fingertips, and we haven't reduced our hours to reflect that.

The Challenges and Problems We Face Now

As I've already mentioned, brain power is different that body power. The body can do eight hours of work, but almost none of us can really focus intensely on mentally intensive work for eight hours a day.

Again, the eight-hour workday was set up for the *body*, not the mind.

There are plenty of studies out there that are trying to answer the question, "How many minutes in a row should a person work before taking a break?" The fact that they're even doing these studies should show you that trying to work for eight hours makes no sense.

But just for the record, it's 52 minutes. Just 52 minutes of work before your brain is shot, and it needs to be followed by a 17 minute break. That's what the most recent study found, from a productivity company behind the popular application Desktime.

It makes sense, because in the knowledge worker world, it's all about managing *mental* energy.

How Tech-Savvy Workers Take Advantage of This Mess

Let's take a look at the types of workers who are doing well in this new environment, and really taking advantage of a world that their employers don't understand.

Part of the reason I understood the validity of the five-hour workday is because that's about the amount of time I was spending in the office. It wasn't purposefully five hours a day, and it just wasn't a rigid schedule. I'd just come in, knock out a project, and get out of there. I was putting in probably two to three good hours of work, with all the less productive stuff mixed in, like talking with people and taking breaks.

If you think about it from an employer's perspective, you're not buying physical labor from knowledge workers, You're buying their outputs. And how long it takes them to make that product is irrelevant.

Work is force multiplied by distance. Distance is time, and let's assume that's the variable that can't be changed. But force? That can absolutely be changed. You can ratchet that up and down, and when force goes up, you're getting the same work done in a shorter period of time. Agreed?

The movie *Good Will Hunting* starts out with a professor throwing down a challenge problem to his class of MIT whiz kids. He puts a complex math problem on the chalkboard in the hallway and says he hopes someone in the class can prove it by the end of the semester. It's apparently a really hard problem that only he and a group of Nobel Laureates have solved as part of this MIT class challenge.

Will, played by Matt Damon, is the janitor from the wrong side of town and not someone in the class. He sees the problem while mopping up the floor one day and solves it in a couple minutes. No one knows who solved it, so the professor puts a harder problem up. A problem that took he and the MIT staff two years to collectively solve. Will sees that a few days later, and solves it again in just a few minutes but gets caught by the professor, and the rest of the movie is about the professor trying to get this kid to realize his massive potential.

That movie is a great example of what's happening today

in the knowledge worker world. You're paying people to solve problems. Some people have the ability to solve very complex problems, very quickly. At the end of the day, the question really is, "How much work got done?" It shouldn't be: "How long did people work today?" That's not the right question anymore.

From a strategic business perspective, you're actually hiring knowledge workers for the quality of their minds. The truth is, you can have brilliant people in your office for five hours a day, but those most talented minds are actually working 24 hours a day for you.

They're always thinking, always solving problems for your business. They're thinking about it in the shower, they're having ideas in the middle of the night. And when those genius minds are well taken care of, and well-rested, they are unleashed and explosively productive.

You're not paying knowledge workers for eight hours a day of their time. You're paying them for a year of value provided to your business. Hours are irrelevant, if value and solutions exceed the cost of the employee. But there will be little value of any employee, when their brains are destroyed by an excessive workday.

If you understand this, and believe it, it will help you take this leap of faith to a five-hour workday.

Your company's biggest concern should be how to get the most talented people on your team. All of your energy should be focused on solving that problem, because that's the key to solving the rest of your business problems. How do you get those people?

You offer them something that few others are offering them, but something that they most certainly deserve, for accomplishing their work faster than average workers do.

You give talented knowledge workers *time*. You give them their time back.

Don't they deserve that?

Methods That Try to Provide Work-Life Balance, But Don't Quite Work

Since most employees have realized that they're a lot more productive now, they've manufactured some creative attempts to renegotiate a better deal for themselves. The eight-hour day, for some reason, has been sacred and untouchable.

As a result, employees have creatively invented ways to get around that problem, and we'll look at these common work-arounds next. The problem is that none of these inventions are a good deal for *both* the employer and the employee, and I'll explain why.

Telecommuting

Telecommuting is the most common work-life strategy that is spreading like wildfire. It's another newly-enabled part of life, thanks to many of the technologies we've discussed. There are many jobs that can now be done from anywhere, thanks to the internet and our mobile devices.

Technology has made it very easy for me to work from anywhere. And as an employee, it certainly does buy you freedom. If you have kids, it's especially helpful, and that's a major influence behind many people's desire to telecommute.

Many aspects of telecommuting make perfect sense. You're allowing people to work at home, and negotiating a better deal for them (or so they believe). But in my opinion, I think it's not the ideal solution for productivity. We don't telecommute in our company, because our five-hour workday makes us very, very productive in the office.

I've run my own businesses from home over the years, and from offices. I'm much more productive in the office, for all the obvious reasons. It's easy to get distracted at home, because that's your place of rest and enjoyment. Your kids are there, your dogs are there, and there's nobody to keep you on task but yourself.

This new world of knowledge work is a game of focus. This new world is about optimizing the mind. You want a work environment where you can eliminate as many potential distractions as you want, and for most people, home is not the ideal environment. But there are other reasons that an office is better.

To really advance your business in this era (and the world of the future), you need the newly-coined concept of "idea sex." You need your team to always be brainstorming, sharing ideas, and not necessarily in a formal way.

At Tower, it's common that I'll have an idea, and mention it to someone else on the team. We might riff on it for a minute, and then they'll carry it elsewhere, where someone else will develop that idea further. And it's completely informal, just part of the natural processes of being in an office environment.

In the old days, innovations were planned, and less frequent. Companies would have a big, wasteful meeting to come up with ideas. But today, innovation is a constant. We move forward not because of one huge idea, but thousands of small ones that happen constantly. It's built into the culture of successful companies in the knowledge working world. It *has* to be, or you're going to be out of business.

The daily interactions that happen in an office environment are one of the biggest benefits to knowledge workers, especially if you get a lot of really smart people who have different areas of expertise working together in the same environment. That's an environment where ideas can have sex and reproduce in large numbers.

When you go to telecommuting, you no longer get these random-but-consistent innovations. You don't get the benefits of these well-designed, open offices where everybody's in the same room. Where you might have an idea and it's very easy to just lean over and mention it to a teammate.

If you're working from home, what happens if you have an

idea? That idea would need to be emailed or texted to a team-mate. There's more risk in that. What if this is a stupid idea? What if it gets forwarded and now it's more work for me? What if, what if, what if.

And it's more time drained, sending an email that nobody's expecting you to send. And that's why fewer ideas are voiced by telecommuters. It's just a completely different environment that does not facilitate group innovation.

Because of all the recent productivity gains, telecommuting became the answer to the question that talented employees find themselves thinking every day in their offices: why am I spending eight hours in a day in this office, when I really only do two or three hours of work?

So (using the instructions in *The Four Hour Workweek* to negotiate telecommuting), the most talented employees are get-ting themselves out of these longer-than-necessary workdays by getting out of the office *entirely*. Once home, they are free to do their two to three hours of work, take the rest of the day off, and nobody knows the difference.

But I see it everyday, and I feel it everyday myself as a knowl-edge worker: we're all much happier, more innovative, more productive, and more successful coming into the office and working for five hours per day. It's the perfect compromise, if everyone goes home a little after 1:00 p.m. It provides workers with the same amount of free time they'd get if they were tele-commuting, and it provides the businesses with the benefits of having talented people working together in one office.

Flex Time: A Hidden Killer

Flex time is another new attempt at giving employees a better work-life balance, and it's twice as terrible as telecommuting.

In extreme cases of flex time, businesses essentially don't have set working hours. If somebody likes working at night, they can come in and work at night. If somebody likes taking five hours off in the middle of the day, they can do that. This all of a sudden makes it really hard to track when people are coming, when people are going, and nobody really knows how long anybody is there in the offices.

I think this is just another version of the idea behind telecommuting, that give talented and productive workers a way to enjoy the fruits of their productivity by getting out of the office. But this one is even worse, because nobody knows when anybody will be there, and communication cycles (and the projects that depend on them) essentially work as if everyone is telecommuting. It just shifts to email-centric communication, and there's no idea sex.

I look at our business like a football team. Everybody's got to be on the field at the same time, for us to accomplish our best. You've got to know you can count on your teammates to be there, and perform, and inspire you to perform at your highest level too. And from an operational standpoint, flex time is like having six players on the field instead of 11.

Whether it's offense (innovating and moving projects forward), or it's defense (customer service, emergencies), you've got to have your full team on the field if you want to win. As soon as you go to these flex times, it's a real problem because the assembly line of today comes to a complete stop, several times a day.

Here's how you'll know when the assembly lines of today come to a screeching halt. It's when someone says something like this: "Okay, well that's something that Julie will have to handle, and she's not here for five more hours. I'll make a note to go see her when she gets here, and then I'll finish my piece tomorrow when I get back in."

Here's how it sounds when your entire team is on the field: "Hey Jules, can you get me a username for this client to access our product? Sweet, thanks. Just got it, I'll send it over to the client now."

That's how flex time adds 24 hours to a one-minute task. And that's how companies with flex time and telecommuting lose customers and miss project deadlines.

But What About Employees and Work-Life Balance?

Flex time obviously has benefits for workers. If they have a doctor's appointment or something similar that comes up, flex time allows them to work that into their schedules without needing to burn vacation time or sick time. But there's a better solution to this problem.

If your company is like mine, with a five-hour workday that ends at 1:00 p.m., then employees have a four-hour window every single afternoon to take care of all those little things. Especially for people with medical issues that require frequent doctors appointments, but also for people with kids who have multiple appointments to manage, it would be a huge benefit for both the employee and the business.

I think there's a real problem in the typical workplace if there are a handful of people that are often gone during working hours, even if those people maintain a reasonable level of productivity. The problem is that other employees get resentful of it, and feel like there's a bit of unfair favoritism to the employees who have kids, or other reasons that they need to be gone from work so often. This hurts your culture, which hurts your productivity.

And to some degree, the resentful employees are right: it isn't fair. But we haven't had a better solution than flex time, until now.

The Game Within The Game: Faking Work

Because of flex time, and telecommuting, and the ability of talented workers to accomplish their work in three hours per day, there's a new productivity-killing problem inside most of our companies: the game of faking it.

It's the worst in the biggest companies, where middle managers are constantly in a political game of measuring workers' productivity. There's a feeling of guilt from good employees, followed by processes made to be intentionally slow (like slower reporting, or extra meetings), and there are politics surrounding it all.

Flex time and telecommuting really fuel this fire, and workers being gone during working hours really draws extra suspicion from co-workers and managers. It sets the stage for the toxic work culture that destroys productivity.

This game of politics and faking it will continue, for most businesses, because these crafty workarounds have indeed created a very unfair environment in the workplace. The most talented employees figure out how to telecommute, or maximize their flex time, or run a side business while they're at work. But there are no winners and losers here: everyone loses.

Attempting to Drive Productivity With Money and Raises

There's extensive discussion about wages in America right now, as we're long overdue to raise the minimum wage. But that's not going to do anything for work-life balance, happiness, and productivity in the knowledge-working world that this book is primarily focused upon.

Not many knowledge workers are working for the minimum wage, because they're all worth more than that and are generally being paid much more than minimum wage. Henry Ford mentioned this as well when he innovated the workday, saying that he was unlikely to keep any worker who wasn't worth more than the minimum wage.

I'm talking more about workers who (in 2016) are earning on average $25/hour. While minimum wage increases aren't relevant to our discussion, we definitely should talk about whether paying knowledge workers more money will increase productivity.

For some reason, we've had a long-running assumption in our society that more money means more happiness. More money buys more motivation. More money fixes everything.

In 2010, a study of 450,000 working Americans was analyzed by Princeton economist Angus Deaton and psychologist Daniel Kahneman. They analyzed Americans' self-reported happiness levels, and whether there were differences in happiness that could be attributed to income levels.

It's not surprising to any of us that happiness levels rose with income. But here's the statistic that explains why there's a limit to the effectiveness of raises: above an income of $75,000, there were no incremental gains in day-to-day happiness. Going from $35,000 to $75,000 would be a large and significant gain in happiness, but those gains stopped at $75,000.

Once you're making more than $75,000, it's highly likely that you're starting to buy stuff you don't really need. Your basic needs are met, and lots of fun "wants" as well. Remember the Aussie Mindset? Happiness doesn't live in work or possessions, it lives in *time and experiences.* And more money can't equal more time or experiences, if you're held captive at work for 9.4 hours every day.

A Great Example of How Raises Worked (And Could Work Even Better)

At the INC 500 Conference in 2015 I discussed my five-hour workday with a business owner named Dan Price. He runs a payment processing company in Seattle called Gravity Payments, which is likely 100% knowledge workers (programming, customer service, marketing, and more).

Dan read the happiness study I mentioned, but he did much more than that. He took a leap of faith and actually tried it.

On April 13, 2015, he gathered his 120 employees and announced that everyone—including himself—would be earning $70,000. For Dan, it would be a massive pay cut, but for most of the employees, it was a significant raise. A firestorm ensued in the media.

On one side, there were fearful business owners and conservative people like Rush Limbaugh, who said, "I hope this company is a case study in MBA programs on how socialism does not work, because it's gonna fail."

On the other side, there were many others celebrating what Dan did, as a sign of how CEOs and business owners should be sharing the profits gained from today's productivity. In 2013, the average American CEO was paid *331 times more* than their average workers, according to a study of 3,000 corporations by Aflcio.org.

There are two reasons that moving his company's minimum wage to $70,000 per year was a brilliant move for Dan. On one hand, he was thinking about productivity and how to make customers happy. Secondly, and something I'd say is a direct tie to customer happiness for most companies, is that he wanted to take care of his employees. Not just because he felt it was the right thing to do, but also because the company's growth and survival was dependent on employees' ability to make customers happy.

When I talked to Dan, I remember that it was his essence and his priority to operate in this way. He's the kind of person who would think, "If I can't run a business and pay people enough money to make them truly happy, then I don't want to run a business. And I'll just run this thing into the ground if I can't do this."

And so he took the leap of faith and tried it. He had the presence of mind to know that it hadn't really been tried yet, and he had the guts to try. How did it turn out?

Six months later, when Inc.com ran a story updating the progress of the company, the results were in. Before the pay raise announcement, his company was receiving about 30 customer inquiries (leads) per month. In the first two weeks after the raise, his company got over 2000 inquiries.

Customers will reward businesses that treat their employees well. For Dan's company, they received a ton of media coverage and that was key to the increase in inquiries, but those customers were also showing their support.

This goes back to a TED Talk I heard years ago by Simon Sinek, titled, "How great leaders inspire action." It's got over 25 million YouTube views. In it, he emphasized that people buy from you because they *believe* the same things that you believe. It's not just that you have a great product, but it's the very simple statement, "Hey, I like that company. They believe what I believe, they're taking care of their employees, and they're ahead of their time. I'm going to buy from them."

In addition to the huge increase in customer inquiries, the following has happened for Dan's company:

- Profits have *doubled*.
- Retention rate of employees was high: 118 of 120 employees stayed.
- Retention of clients went from "amazing" to "more amazing." The industry average is a 68% retention rate, and they were already hitting 91% as a company. But now they're at 95%. That's incredible for any industry (especially payment processing), and that's what happens when happy workers keep customers happy.

I really applaud Dan and what he's doing here, and I told him that at the INC 500 conference. Hearing the story of what he did, during the same time I was contemplating the five-hour workday, really helped me take action. I still believe that the five-hour workday is a better overall solution for productivity and happiness, but I love what Dan is doing because at least he is trying *something*. At least he's seeing the problems and experimenting toward the solutions that work for both employees and employers.

The better solution here, I believe, would be to pay workers well *and* reduce their workday. You're paying them $70,000 and they have enough to live comfortably, and that's certainly improved their happiness levels, which would help drive productivity gains. But here's the thing: they're still only going to accomplish two to three hours of real work in a day.

But if you give employees the $70,000 *and* give them back a huge chunk of their time, then you've had a massive and lasting positive effect on their life. At that point, quality of life skyrockets, and productivity does too.

Tomorrow's Productivity Requires Us to Drop the "Guilt Factor"

I was just listening to Gary Vaynerchuk, a very popular and respected thought leader in today's business world. He's a true entrepreneur, and I'm a huge fan of his and have followed him for years. He rose to prominence by starring in his own online show about wine, which was a contributing factor to growing his online wine business to a multi-million dollar level. He became one of the earliest internet marketing celebrities, and remains a thought leader in the realm of marketing and business strategy for the modern age.

Gary often writes about and speaks about the importance of hustle and hard work, and his widely acknowledged goal is to buy the New York Jets football team. So the goal that's being shown by his example is that his goal of work is to amass five billion dollars, so he can buy the thing he really wants. That's his goal, and he works around the clock in pursuit of it.

That's the "hustler" mentality, and he talks about it often. He works 12-hour days, or maybe 17-hour days. On one of Gary's recent podcasts, a listener posed the question, "What do you do if you've lost the hustle? How do you get back on track?"

To answer the question, Gary went through a few ideas, but then he went on to say how much he enjoyed the holiday season, because it was a time when business slows down and he didn't feel guilty for not working.

Guilty for not working. This is the problem I see. This is the Protestant work ethic lingering in our brains.

Gary Vaynerchuk is incredibly successful, and he's likely worth millions of dollars. More importantly, he is doing exactly what he loves to do. He does the entrepreneurial hustle because that's what he'd do even if he wasn't being paid, you see. Financially, he doesn't need to hustle if he doesn't want to. He certainly doesn't need to feel *guilty* for not working. But he does.

You shouldn't have to feel guilty for not working. You get to choose what you do in this life, for the most part. But in the current American culture, we seem to myopically be defined by how hard we work, and how much money we accumulate over the period of our lives. Those are the badges of honor, in that belief system.

Not everyone is like Gary Vaynerchuk. Not everyone has the same interests, hobbies, and passions as Gary Vaynerchuk. And the important thing to understand is that this is okay. Gary uses his free time to do exactly what he loves around the clock, just as you should be able to do. His hobby just happens to be building businesses and talking about building businesses. He's really good at it.

I share similar interests to Gary and many other true entrepreneurs. If I have a free weekend, oftentimes I'll be in the office working on my latest business development project or thinking up new businesses. That's my hobby. Maybe I'm a little weird, but I dream about this stuff. I see it as a creative outlet.

I work a five-hour day, and then do whatever the hell I want. But sometimes, that's working some more. It's no different than if I loved to paint and that's how I spent my free time. Or if I loved to surf. Or if I loved to write. Or if I loved to coach little league. I'm not watching the clock when I'm doing my hobby. I'm doing it until I'm exhausted and just have to eat or sleep.

My business partner Mark Cuban is like Gary, although he's already arrived at his destination—he owns the NBA team he loves. And you know what? He still works on developing businesses around the clock because he too loves it and is good at it. He sees business as a sport. He's a billionaire, so clearly he doesn't have to do anything he doesn't really want to do. The thing is, it's his hobby. This is play to him. He would do it if he wasn't paid to do it.

But none of this means that everyone in our society should aspire to be like Gary Vaynerchuk or Mark Cuban. That's not the only path to a happy and fulfilling life. Not everyone is good at developing businesses or even good at making money. Who cares? Most people are probably far better, and far more interested in other pursuits, than developing businesses or making money. People have different passions and different talents, and a productive, healthy society is one that lets everyone pursue what they love and what they are good at. Not all of those things produce income, but they do enhance the quality of life for themselves and those around them.

This is what the five-hour workday is about. Getting the "have to" work done as quickly and efficiently as possible, and then unlocking this other productivity of society that is largely hidden and repressed today.

Why Time Is Becoming the New Motivator, Not Money

It's the simplified belief system that I have a problem with. That's why I look at what Dan Price has done with the $70,000 salaries, and I see how it definitely helps to make people happier and more productive.

But what if there's a different belief system that would lead us to something even better? Something that money cannot buy?

The object of work, to me, is to increase the quality of someone's life. That's the idea, or none of us would work. We're pursuing a better life. And that better quality of life certainly does involve how much money you earn, up to that $75,000 threshold mentioned in the 2010 study.

But quality of life is also about the *relationships* you have. It's about the *experiences* in life, the interests you pursue when you're not working. True happiness is not one-dimensional, and can't be entirely driven by a one-dimensional solution (like a $75,000 salary). Our capitalistic society has become very one-dimensional, and you see the problems of that in the people who are rising to the top, with one strong dimension and no balance in life beyond that one dimension.

For example, there are very wealthy people in Silicon Valley committing suicides at an alarming rate. Their whole reason for moving to Silicon Valley, I assume, is because they want to be successful (according to the American definition of success). They want to start a business, be powerful, sell their business, and live happily ever after.

When this is the one and only goal for a person, it can end disastrously. There's a very good chance they'll achieve that "success," and buy their Ferrari and big houses, but find that they're not really fulfilled. Because relationships and experiences and personal growth have all been sacrificed along the way, and it turns out, those building blocks of happiness matter much more than money.

Hence, these "successful" people—finding their lives to be completely unfulfilling, and knowing no other narrative of success—are committing suicide. It's crazy, and this problem alone should be evident that maybe we're *all* looking at the wrong goals here, when it comes to why we're working and how we're living.

More Than Ever, The Better Life Needs Time

At my company, I feel that I pay everyone well and distribute profits fairly, but for me, that's not the sole reason I'm running a business. It's not my sole focus to get every worker up to the magical $75,000 pay rate. My goal is to answer this question: "How do I create a better life for my employees and myself? How do I drive growth in business, in a way that provides a better life for all of us?"

That's what the five-hour workday is really about. You're paying everyone fairly and driving happiness in that way, but more importantly, you're also *giving them their life back*. Everyone is getting a fair wage that allows them to live comfortably, and they're also getting the time necessary to pursue a better overall life.

This combination, in our experience at Tower, has skyrocketed people's happiness and their gratitude for having their job. And it's much deeper than it sounds. It's more than money, more than being off a few hours early. It's what this job is *empowering* in the rest of our lives.

Instead of your life being focused on your job, and your job consuming most of your time, everything becomes reversed by a five-hour workday. Your *life* becomes the focus. Your job is now the valuable tool that gives you the money to pursue the better life you want, and your job also gives you the *time* needed to experience that life on a daily basis.

Getting off work at 1:00 p.m. does not just open up an incremental amount of time, it opens up three times the amount of free time. Imagine getting off at 1:00 p.m. every weekday. You'd probably have so much time that you'd be bored. You'd have to invent activities for yourself, but you get to pick what they are. That's the whole point. It's no different than what I did with my college buddies every day for three months on our backpacking trip across Australia. And I can tell you that was extraordinary living like most people will never experience before they die.

Why Business Owners Are Scared of This, But Shouldn't Be

I know that many business owners are really scared to try this, and it's the primary reason I'm writing this book. I want to identify where that fear comes from, and what shift in mentality is required in order to take this leap into the future.

Many business owners, whether they'd say it aloud or not, want their employees' lives to be focused on their jobs. Focused on the company, more than their own lives outside of work. But this is no longer going to work with talented knowledge workers. Those days are gone, and it's going to take the exact opposite perspective to unlock true productivity from this point forward.

A strategy that focuses solely on money isn't enough for employees' happiness and productivity. Time is the new money.

A strategy that offers flex time and telecommuting aren't enough for the business' productivity and culture. In-person teamwork drives the most innovation and productivity gains.

The combination of those two truths gives us one magic bullet: the shorter workday.

Ahead of the Curve, or Behind It: Your Choice

The productivity tools that have changed our world haven't changed anything about the money paid to workers. They've only changed the time it takes to accomplish our work. We need to accept that truth, and treat time differently. Because our businesses all depend on it.

In the long term, I believe every business in the knowledge working world will be dealing with the reality of a shorter workday. This is inevitable. Smart businesses expedite the inevitable to gain advantage. You can either be ahead of this curve and enjoy the advantages, or behind it and suffer the consequences.

The productivity tools have freed up a massive chunk of our day, and more profits along the way, and virtually none of this new surplus in time or money have been shared with workers.

But talented workers know it already (or they do now, by reading this book), and they're going to pursue their share of the gains.

Right now, most businesses are looking at productivity gains (from a time perspective) and saying, "Okay, we just saved two hours a day thanks to this new software. Let's double down, keep working hard for nine hours a day, and send more profits to the top."

With that time saved, you could be taking your life back. You could be giving free time back to your employees and fostering an environment of productivity-seeking employees. But few companies are doing that.

In starting and running my business, and really deciding even what business to go into, I've looked at how hundreds of other entrepreneurs run their businesses, and the purposes behind their actions. I quickly came to the conclusion that smart people have the luxury of either creating a business that adds something to society, or creating one that is merely a parasite on society. You can build products and services that truly enhance people's lives, just as you can manipulate people into buying something they don't need or is bad for them and society.

There is a lot of money to be made in being a parasite. People who obsess about scarcity think about the world this way: kill or be killed. If I win, someone has to lose. There's a lot of money in cigarettes, for instance. Same for payday loans—preying on poor, uneducated people—there's great money in that. Hedge funds make a lot of money by simply taking it from someone else, some investors less sophisticated than them. Illegal drugs, now that's a profitable business. Almost as much as in legal pharmaceuticals that are pushed on people that don't need them. There are great returns in slavery, too, but that's not a reason to go that route.

But there are also great ways to provide value. People who understand the concept of abundance understand this. This is how economies grow, how trade creates wealth, and how societies evolve. The more value you create, the more your contribution will be rewarded. There is plenty of money to be made in truly adding to society. In organizing the world's information, or in creating technology that is also beautiful. In creating the future of greener energy. There's even decent money in creating something very simple like stand up paddle boards, which help people explore nature, go on adventures, and have fun experiences with their friends and family, while also getting in shape.

When I began hiring employees, I realized it's not just about what your company does, but who is inside working at that company and what you can do for them. I began to feel partially responsible for my employees and their happiness. I realized that this is the point where business owners' philosophies force them to make a choice: to care about your employees, or to not care about your employees. You can choose to add value here, or you can choose to be a parasite, just as with your company objective.

Add value or be a parasite. You can do either one of those. It's a very easy choice, but one you consciously need to make, if you want to take the path of adding value.

I can take the path of the parasite, and sadly, that's probably the easiest and most societally acceptable path for a business owner to take in America's current working culture. I can have a business that focuses solely on profits and maximizing shareholder returns. A business that cares about employees only as much as the lawyers and human resources advisors say it needs to, to avoid lawsuits and excessive turnover.

On this path, I'd essentially be choosing to suck the blood out of everything around me, by taking all the gains in money and gains in time for my own benefit. And in doing so, I can send the message that my happiness and quality of life, as the business owner, is more important than everyone else's. Few employees would complain, since this is currently normal in America.

Or, I can take the path of figuring out a creative way to add value. I can run a business in a way that it actively focuses on creating a great life for everyone involved in the business. That's the type of business that feels like a family, where the business owners clearly take action toward providing a better life for everyone involved: the customers, employees, and shareholders. Where productivity gains are shared among everyone, instead of siphoned to the top.

Again, either path is available to you now, in the short term. The tougher but smarter choice is to figure out how to add value, and it's the path I'm taking with my company. The easier choice is to be a parasite, and it seems like many companies are choosing that path. But what happens next on that path, I believe, makes it the worst choice.

Everyone is connected now, online, so it's only a matter of time before the most talented people hear that there's a better deal for them. Only a matter of time before they jump ship, for the better life that simply isn't possible when parasites take all the gains in money and time (but especially the gains in time).

This is part of what Henry Ford meant in his interview, when he said, "These are the cold, hard facts of business today." And I think Henry would say the same thing about the decision we have now. Even if you want to stop what's coming, I don't believe you can.

Employees and business owners alike will begin whispering, "Hey, we're only working two to three hours a day here, and we're more productive than your company. That's why your company is losing its best workers to mine, and that's why you're losing market share too."

I didn't create this future. I'm just delivering the news.

I believe a shorter workday is inevitable, and it's already happening in many hidden ways. The question is: do you want to ride this wave with a happy and productive team? Or do you want to fight this wave on your own, and drown in the riptide?

Chapter Five

THE GOLDEN AGE OF ENTREPRENEURSHIP

———

I JUST DID AN INTERVIEW WITH INC. MAGAZINE FOR THEIR article about the state of small business, and I was joined by several other entrepreneurs whose companies were one of the 500 fastest-growing companies in America. It shocked me, how many people in the top 500 companies were pessimistic about the current economy, government, and future.

Maybe I look at this world a little differently than most business owners. When the writer asked me about various obstacles mentioned by other business owners, my reply was essentially, "What are you talking about? This is the golden age of entrepreneurship."

It truly is the best time in the history of the world to start a business. Even if access to loans through banks is difficult—and it is indeed non-existent, for most startups—we still have all of these amazing productivity tools that have never been available until now. Even the most basic off-the-shelf software would've taken you hundreds of thousands of dollars to get access to, just a few short years ago.

Today, and tomorrow, you can test an idea and new business with very little money. You can start a blog and your own media company for *free*. You can put up an e-commerce site, pay $29.95 a month, and you have the same technology that Amazon.com is using.

I guess I have a different perspective because in my journey of entrepreneurship, I've tried a bunch of businesses that failed. That's what everyone should be doing, because the cost of starting a business is very small compared to the upside of what happens if your idea gets traction and enjoys success.

Along the way, I've really changed how I look at work. The idea of living and working have meshed together for me, and it all just feels like living. That's not because I'm working 80 hours a week, either. It's because I do a little bit of work on most days, and because I'm well-rested and enjoying an overall balance of life beyond work, that little bit of daily work is actually quite enjoyable to me.

When I meet many of today's successful entrepreneurs at conferences and other events, I find this commonality exists in much the same way for them. We're all brainstorming with each other about what's working, talking about our projects and ideas, and blending that in with our fun. There's a balance there, and that balance drives the type of productivity that's needed now.

The Type of Business Owners Who Are Thriving Right Now

In the past few years, I've become especially observant of many ultra-successful entrepreneurs who are thriving in this new information age. I want to understand not only what types of tools they're using, but also what type of business and overall life they're building with their time and money.

Before long, one commonality became very apparent: the

ultra-successful, optimistic, thriving entrepreneurs were automating everything they could in their business. They were leveraging new technologies and processes to become hyper-efficient, hyper-effective people. Every single one of them.

That only brings us to the point where they've got a profitable, successful business. My deeper question was, what do these people do with this new superpower of hyper-efficiency? Do they start working 80 hours a week, so they can make $100 million instead of only $10 million?

Some of them might do that, but for the most part, most of them don't. Most of these ultra-successful entrepreneurs choose to pursue something beyond money. They choose an extraordinary life.

Underground Mavericks

One of the conferences I've attended is called The Internet Underground, and it's for these type of entrepreneurs who are finding hacks and using internet technologies to grow businesses exponentially quickly.

Yanik Silver is the person who was running this annual conference for a couple thousand people, and it was very beneficial for me. These types of people are happy to share strategies, and exchange ideas, and form new ones.

On the side, he started a smaller group called the Mavericks. This was a group of adventure-seekers, with millions of dollars in earnings and a desire to get together for adventure trips. They went to Russia to fly MiG fighter jets, they went to Baja to do the Baja 500, and they did all kinds of crazy stuff.

Last year, I went to a summer camp for entrepreneurs, and it was just an incredible idea. You're back to being a kid again, bunking up with other people. You've got fun activities spread throughout the week, and you're learning from each other along the way, all day and all night. It was a blast.

Those are the types of things that the successful entrepreneurs of the information age are doing. They're asking themselves how to make life more interesting and fun, and they're pursuing that life. And why shouldn't they? Why shouldn't we all do this?

The other thing they're doing is that they're minimizing work, the way the ancient Greeks did. When they're working, they're working. They're very focused. And the minute that work is done, they get the hell out of there.

I can say this for myself, when it was just a one man show with my poker chip business for about five years, I did the same. I experienced the benefits of this life, and learned to minimize my work to maximize my life. I had a shop that people could come visit, but when my work was done, I closed the shop. I didn't leave a note on the door. I just left.

For the successful and highly-efficient entrepreneurs, it's all about productivity. These are small companies, or one-person operations with outsourced help, and there's no politics. Nobody to impress. Nobody to turn in a weekly report to. So of course, there's no reason to waste time at work. No reason to turn three hours of work into 9.4 hours of wasted time on Earth.

They've taken this new reality, and focused on creating a great quality of life. Is it any surprise then, that if they grow their companies and add employees, they want this same quality of life for their entire team?

Is it any surprise that their employees are encouraged to leverage the same productivity tools, and discover new ones? If the benefit is quality of life, and time, then everyone has a strong incentive to innovate. Everyone shares the fruits of hyper-efficiency.

Lean Lions Instead of Fat Cats

When I was a kid, I got a job bussing tables at the local yacht club. I worked my way up to bartender and that's how I financed my way through college and travel. My image of a successful and happy man would be someone who owned a business, became rich, drove a fancy car, got a fat yacht, had a big house, drank fancy drinks, and golfed every day. He'd be overweight from eating extravagantly, he'd smoke fine cigars, wear suits, and have that overall look and attitude of superiority. The "fat cats" of old, you might say.

But this new breed of successful entrepreneurs are almost completely different than these "fat cats" of old. They're using their time freedom to exercise, and they're almost all in pretty good physical shape. They're in t-shirts and jeans, not suits. They have very good relationships, and very healthy lives over-all. The definition of success is now becoming something that goes beyond maximizing money, for these business owners and their entire teams. I've been really surprised, until these past few years, because I'd always thought there had to be tradeoffs. That you could be a gym rat, or have a successful business. You could have good relationships, or have a good career.

But today's successful entrepreneurs and their companies are showing us that we can have it all. They are basically already operating in this five-hour workday world. It was like peering into the future.

It makes sense in retrospect, because the same sort of mind-set and discipline used in maximizing productivity could also be used to maximize physical strength, relationships, and any other aspect of life. When I adopted this same mindset toward leverage and efficiency, I realized, "Holy shit. I can actually can do both. I don't have to pick one or the other."

This, to me, is the new definition of success. The ability to pursue *both* quality of life and success in business. This is only a reality now, because becoming successful in business doesn't require all of your time, or your employees' time either.

To believe this and understand how it's possible, let's look at some strategies that are now being leveraged to manage our energy and drive higher productivity and innovation.

Cycling Your Energy Toward a Productive Balance

One strategy I've recently learned is a concept called cycling. This is as much about avoiding burnout as it is about driving productivity, but it could be argued that the world of today requires both.

Let's say you're looking at three aspects of your life that you want to feel successful about: your financial wellbeing, your physical health, and the quality of your relationships. These would be common pillars of focus for many people currently.

The problem here is that each of those pillars are difficult to give your full focus to, in a balanced way. When you start trying focus on all of those at the same time, it can be tough to maintain your energy level and make progress in any of them.

So, to manage their energy and avoid burning out completely, I've seen entrepreneurs engage in this process they call cycling. They'd take four months and give their primary focus to their business. Then the next four months, they'd take an active focus on their physical health and strength, while running their business in a much less energy-intensive way.

Then they'd take four months and give the majority of their time and energy to their relationships. If they had families, this would mean more time with their kids or spouse. If they were single, it means spending more time dating, building new relationships, strengthening old friendships.

Then repeat. It's managing all three important aspects of life, but giving each piece an intense focus at varying points, to stay in balance and manage energy. Avoiding burnout and optimizing your energy is crucially important in the knowledge working world.

The five-hour workday works beautifully for cycling, and

gives people more time to focus on these other important elements of life. It allows for more balance between all the elements at any given time, too. Your family and friends would likely never feel neglected if you limited your work to five hours per day, and you could still squeeze in some daily exercise too.

The only reason the term "burnout" even exists, is because of the 9.4 hour workday, and the 50+ hour workweek.

But What If I Occasionally Enjoy a Long Day's Work?

That doesn't mean that you can't or shouldn't work the occasional 12-hour days, if you want to or need to. That's why the whole idea of cycling dovetails really nicely with the five-hour workday. You can change your focus to work if you need to, and still return to that five-hour workday later, when it's time to shift the focus away from work.

I completely understand that there are periods of the year that are busier than others, and especially if you enjoy your work (or simply don't hate it), that working a long day feels right and is right. I fall into this category, because I love building businesses, so I'm a person who actually likes those long days to a certain degree at times.

The fact is that certain people are more capable of doing high-level, concentrated knowledge work over longer periods of time than others. They were born with stronger, more endurance-friendly minds, or they've developed them. It's no different than certain people who are physically stronger than others or have more physical endurance than others. Some people run marathons for fun, without their body breaking down.

Mark Cuban can work around the clock and keep tabs on 100 companies. Elon Musk has built an entire company of these types of people for SpaceX and they are doing amazing things. Silicon Valley has small teams of these types and they are able to do amazing things too. Many of the people that I employ at

Tower are of this nature and they see the five-hour workday as what it is: just a baseline. But not everyone can run marathons, and it's stupid to have marathon running as a national sport that everyone is expected to do and enjoy.

I've come to realize that balance is important, especially when I'm responsible for leading a team to victory, not just managing to get there myself. As an entrepreneur with pretty good endurance, I can actually put my head down and get my life way out of balance. I've found I need to be cautious of trying to run too fast and for too long.

That's why I force myself to cycle out of those periods of work focus and into the other areas of life, in order to maintain my overall energy and productivity in the long term. That's why I try to force myself to take a three-week sabbatical every year to travel to some exotic place. In the past four years, I've gone on extended trips to Cambodia, Vietnam, Thailand, Colombia, South Africa, Zimbabwe, and Botswana, all while running this fast-growing business. I credit those "interruptions" largely with driving my continued success.

Cycling Your Focus and Energy Within Each Day

In knowledge work, you've not only got to think about managing energy levels in the mid-term and long-term, but also within each day. This is where you're looking at your individual workday and breaking down the hours into their ideal portions and functions. You're answering these questions:

- What time of day am I going to work?
- How hard do I typically work during this time of day, compared to others? Why?
- Are there critical tasks that are best done at a certain hour of day, based on communications or operations?
- What times would be ideal for me to work in some breaks?

Most people are more alert and productive in the morning. A January 2015 article by the Harvard Business Review revealed that the most mentally-alert time of day is 11 a.m., and it's a spike that begins a few hours before, and crashes to its lowest point at 3:00 p.m., for most people.

This is why my company has picked the sweet spot in this range, from 8 a.m. to 1:00 p.m., and we don't lose productive time to the typical American lunch hour. We eat lunch after we're done working for the day, so the post-lunch food coma and 3:00 p.m. mental downtime can occur on the beach, or at the gym, or going on a bike ride with our kids.

Nationwide, the typical schedule is a huge productivity-killer. Noon, according to the aforementioned study, is only one hour after our peak of productivity, and it's three hours before our 3:00 p.m. crash. And not only do we lose an hour at lunch, but many dieticians might remind you that a common American meal is high-carb, high-sugar, large-portion. And you know what comes after that: food coma.

Now, from 1:00 p.m. to 2:00 p.m., you've got the delays of settling back into your rhythm at work, and you've got a food coma on top of those delays. So you just lost another hour. And that leaves us with 2:00 p.m. to 3:00 p.m., which is the final descent into the daily crash. Lunch costs us at least one productive hour, but more likely, *two or three* productive hours.

Lunch is also a breeding ground for more culture-killing politics and one-upping of each other. We've all worked with the person who never takes lunch, and makes you feel guilty for taking a break. That person might indeed be more productive by skipping lunch, but working for eight hours straight with no breaks is beyond unhealthy in the knowledge working world. Eliminating lunch and leaving at 1:00 p.m. makes a lot more sense to me, and it's one less opportunity for office politics and burnout.

Artificial Constraints Lead to Genuine Gains

Artificial time constraints are another powerful method that I see being implemented by hyper-productive people. Similar to a business becoming more creative when they have less of a budget, employees become more creative when they have less time.

If you reduce the number of hours you have to dedicate towards a task, it magically leads you to thinking of new ways to get it done. A classic example of this is finals week in college.

In the typical four-year, full-time college, students all have too much time on their hands. There's a lot of enjoying life and relaxing all year, then you get to finals week and everything changes. All of the sudden, all of these very intelligent and capable people get serious. They accomplish more in that week than the month previous, and it helps them realize that this is possible anytime.

That's why I remember being in school and often having a big project due, putting it off until the last minute, and then accomplishing all of it in a 24-hour period. Everybody around me seemed to be doing the same, and we all knew that it seemed easier and more efficient to knock out all that work in the final 24 hours.

That's an artificial time constraint. You're shortening the allotted window of time for a task, in order to maximize productivity toward that task.

When you go from an eight-hour workday to a five-hour workday, you'll be impressed by what people accomplish. In fact, you can test it tomorrow, with your own productivity.

Try to accomplish your work tomorrow in five hours, and look for all the ways you could save three hours (assuming you're working an 8+ hour day). The first place to start, for most people, is your email inbox.

Email's Evolution: Originally a Godsend, Now a Silent Killer

Tim Ferriss talks about email extensively in *The Four Hour*

Workweek, and for good reason. Email has helped us become more productive in many ways, but we're at a tipping point where it's the next thing that we really need to address as a massive time-waster.

If, like many knowledge workers, you've become a reactive email user—where your email is open all day, and you're responding to every email immediately—then this is where you're likely going to be able to trim an hour or two off of your workday.

A reactive emailer is a slave to everybody else's priorities. They email you, you respond, they email you back again. They're driving your actions. That's why productive people limit their time with email: so they can accomplish more of their own priorities, not other people's.

Try checking email once an hour, then twice a day. You'll experience how this artificial time constraint forces you to batch your emails, and how that saves you time. You won't get interrupted during times of focused (and important) tasks, and people emailing you will solve their own problems before you reply.

Again, you likely have your highest energy levels in the morning, so that's when you should be working on your highest-priority tasks. If you started your day by spending your first three hours on that, and not even checking your email for the first time until 11 a.m. or so, watch how much faster you get through your most important work.

Batching emails made a ton of sense to me when I was reading Ferriss' methods of doing it. I was already batching my orders and shipments, as an e-commerce company. I would never consider packing and shipping each individual order immediately, that would be a complete productivity killer. So why not apply the same method? That was a breakthrough for me.

The Next Constraint: Batching Faster

The next constraint you can test is reducing the time you have for each task that you're batching. Sticking with the email example, an entrepreneur friend of mine named Dan Martell once talked about a great trick he implemented to reduce the time of each email session. He had an old laptop with only a 90-minute battery life, and so his solution was simple: do email at the coffee shop and don't bring a power cord. When the battery dies, I'm done with email.

Another version of this is a fun game I called "racing the UPS guy." When I was running my poker chip business, I was the shipping guy. But I was busy, because I was everything. I was the marketing guy, the product development guy, and the guy who answered the phone. I wanted to reduce my shipping time, to free up time for more important tasks.

Because getting products out the door was really important, I'd come in every day and that would be the first thing I would do. I'd be shipping along, and there were all kinds of interruptions that would slow me down, from phone calls to emails. Before I know it, it's 2:00 p.m. and I'm just finishing shipping. It was very inefficient, and I was making mistakes because of all the interruptions. So one day, I just said screw it, I'm doing this without any interruptions.

Remember the college finals week? That's what I did here, but within the same day. I knew that I could ship 30 packages in two hours, if I wasn't interrupted. I knew that the UPS guy always arrived at 4:00 p.m., so the constraints were defined and ready. I wouldn't start shipping until 2:00 p.m., and I'd force myself to race the UPS guy.

I'd shut down my email, and I wouldn't even answer my cell phone. I was 100% focused on shipping. I knew this UPS guy was coming at 4:00 p.m., and if my buddy called me to chat, I just immediately thought, okay, I can't take this call. This game forced me to focus, and prioritize the task over the interruptions.

It worked. I reduced the total time it took me to ship every day. I instantly became more productive, because I had to be. In the equation of force times distance, I'd greatly increased my force, to compensate for the shorter distance.

By doing that, I basically unlocked 9:00 a.m. to 2:00 p.m., and it felt like magic. It's as if that time was just sitting there before, right in front of me, but I couldn't see it because I was just working inefficiently.

That example is exactly what I think is going on right now, in a hundred different ways, in the typical eight-hour workday. That time is there, and we just haven't created the right constraints that help us see it.

Another Productivity Hack: The Pareto Principle

The Pareto Principle is often called the "80/20 rule." It's the idea that 80% of your productive output comes from 20% of your efforts. Looked at from the standpoint of wasting energy, that same idea means that 80% of your efforts are generating only 20% of your productive output.

This is yet another valuable takeaway that I pulled from *The Four Hour Workweek*. I've mentioned this book enough to you by now that it should come as no surprise that, when we began our five-hour workday at Tower, I had everybody read that book. Our business now depended on understanding that mindset, and living it on a daily basis.

After that, I asked everyone to begin tracking everything they're doing, every day. Write it down, ideally, but at least mentally track it. From there, try to quantify the output of your efforts by time and task. The goal? Identify the 20% of your efforts that are driving 80% of your outputs. Then we can eliminate the wasted efforts, or find ways to make them more productive.

The Ultimate Time Constraint: Absence

Another thing you can implement is a technique called

"management by absence." The idea here is that you just completely stop doing some things, and observe what happens. And nothing is off limits, because your biggest breakthroughs will come from ignoring the tasks you thought were critical.

In my poker chip business, I decided to stop answering the phone while I was shipping. I was scared that if I didn't answer the phone, it would really hurt my business and anger customers. But it didn't, during those two hours I was shipping, as long as I returned calls from voicemail after the UPS guy was gone. So I took it a step further, and batched the times I'd check voicemails and return calls. More time saved, and zero complaints.

Today, I check my voicemails maybe once per month. You'd think that you have to return phone calls, but you really don't need to. It's a choice. Maybe a few things will fall apart, but who cares if a few things fall apart, if all of a sudden you've freed up this massive amount of your time.

I use this same strategy for my personal postal mail. I use a service called Paytrust, which pays all of my bills and collects my important postal mail. They scan and post everything online, then queue it up to be paid with the click of a mouse. I actually only open the rest of my non-essential mail every six months or so.

Again, there can be some fallout here, as on two occasions I've opened mail with a $500+ check in it that was now expired. But it's not about being perfect, it's about saving massive chunks of time. Imagine not opening any mail for six months or even a year. I take this to an extreme, but I truly believe that mail consumes too much of our time. Just because somebody sent it to you, doesn't mean you need to open it.

Bigger Risks, Bigger Gains: Freeing Up Entire Days

As I began to learn all the benefits of batching and absence by management, I started to think about how to apply them during the Christmas holiday season, or anytime I wanted to take a two-week vacation.

Per my usual, I began with an extreme experiment, and I wanted to see what would happen if I simply didn't mail out any orders for an entire two weeks. I sent out messages and called back everyone to tell them their shipment would be delayed.

I don't recommend this as a way to run a business regularly, because predictably, a few people were pissed off. But honestly, it was far fewer people than I expected, and there was valuable learning in this experiment. The other immense value here: two weeks off for vacation and family time. I had enabled more cycling, which would mentally recharge me and enhance my productivity in the mid-term to long-term.

If your business is the type where you could experiment like this, even if for only a day, do it. It's likely that the wheels won't completely fall off, and you'll learn how to batch much of it. For me, I began to ask, "If I can stop shipping for two weeks and the world doesn't end, how can I apply that to productivity?"

So I went from shipping five days a week, to three days a week. No change. I helped by reducing customer expectations in a reasonable way, changing the website shipping verbiage to "We usually ship in one to two business days." It was now the truth, customers knew it, and they didn't care one bit.

Magically, I'd freed up two entire days, from a process standpoint. Two days were completely free of the shipping process, so now I could plan on having two entire days to devote entirely to business development and product development.

In the end, I found that I didn't need those extra two days for the poker chip business, so I did what I do best: started another business. I started *several* other businesses, actually.

The freedom created by these productivity methods are almost unbelievable, when you're experiencing them. I'd just manufactured two days of free time, and I wasn't making any less money, and the customers were just as happy. I wasted years of my life, missing this opportunity. "Holy cow," I remember thinking. "I should have done this a long time ago."

But I couldn't even perceive this was possible, until I gained the knowledge on how to do it, and the guts to take the leap and try it. The knowledge is the easy part, and you've now got that knowledge for yourself. The leap is the scarier half of the equation, but if you'll envision what you'd do with all that extra free time, that should help you make that leap.

From 40 Hours to 12

Long story short, my poker chip business ultimately was reduced from a 40-hour workweek, to a 12-hour workweek. I ended up spending three separate four-hour days on those duties, and this is how I knew a five-hour workday was possible. If I'd stretched that business out across five days, it would've been less than a three-hour workday. This was a one-man business generating $500,000 per year in revenue.

When I started Tower Paddle Boards and got to the point where I needed to hire people, I knew that my team could each accomplish this, because all of their roles were functions I'd done in poker chip company. I'd proven it could be done. That's what helped me take my leap.

This book is for individual workers, freelancers, and entrepreneurs, but I especially want to reach business owners with employees. If you're an employee, I want you to take this to you employer, or drop it on his or her desk. If you're a solo entrepreneur, I want you to read this and have the confidence to create jobs that will leverage you further.

What We Need Next, and Where to Find More Ideas

Here's where it all comes full circle, in the current state of productivity innovations and what I believe is needed next for our companies and society.

Tim Ferriss' *The Four Hour Workweek* changed the game, on an individual level. When he wrote that book and I read it, it was like he was speaking exactly to me, as a solo entrepreneur. There were tens of thousands—if not hundreds of thousands—of entrepreneurs just like me who also read that book, and also felt the same: that Tim had clarified a blueprint of what we were already doing, or thinking of doing. He optimized it all, and took it to the next level, in a way that it could be replicated by everyone.

I felt that *The Four Hour Workweek* was a book for individual entrepreneurs and employees, whether they were currently entrepreneurial-minded employees who simply wanted to get themselves out of the wasteful office, or they were already a solo entrepreneur.

What I'm trying to do now, with the five-hour workday, is carry forward the momentum and apply these same concepts to larger companies. And eventually—when the benefits are fully seen and understood by the masses, when we've all got at least a friend or two working a five-hour workday and we see how their lives are vastly better and fulfilling—then it's my hope that this could become standard across our country and many others.

The Question to Ask

If you haven't read *The Four Hour Workweek* yet, I'd like you to read it after you finish this book. I've explained how I applied many of the book's most powerful methods, but there are many more ideas and applications in there that will open your eyes to what an *individual* could do to leverage technologies to save time.

Then, whether you're an entry-level employee or Fortune 500 CEO, begin to ask yourself one simple question: How would I apply this mindset and these individual tactics to my entire division? Or to my entire company?

When you start asking that question about everything you

work on, and you begin seeing the answers, it will change your life.

Technology: Moving Us From Scarcity to Abundance

A brilliant innovator named Peter Diamandis wrote a book called *Abundance*, which is another book I highly recommend. One of my primary takeaways from this book is the realization that, throughout human history, there were limited resources and slow transfers of knowledge. But today, because of these new technologies, he makes the point that "technology is a resource-liberating mechanism. It can make the once scarce now abundant."

From a business owner's perspective, historically we've all had a mindset of scarcity and zero-sum thinking. If I reduce my workers' total working hours by 50%, I lose 50% of their output and productivity. The workers win, the business loses.

But now, technology enables the opposite. Innovation doesn't slow down, and output is being generated by machines while we sleep. Similar to what Henry Ford did, now it's a game of abundance, where we've got to let go of our fears and trust that a better-rested, more balanced, more productive worker will be able to leverage these tools to their full potential.

That was really the thinking that helped me bridge this mental gap I had, when Tower was working a full eight-hour workday. I read that book and it helped me to think, "No. Tower isn't losing here, it's winning. We can actually reduce our hours, increase our output, and we can grow our company even faster as a result."

The idea of an abundance mindset also helped me trust that there would be different forms of rewards to the business: local and national media coverage (free advertising), our strengthened brand image, our customers' increased purchasing and loyalty, and our ability to attract and retain the most talented employees.

Our New World: Productivity Wisdom From a Facebook Founder

Mark Zuckerberg is the prominent Facebook cofounder who receives the majority of the headlines in the media, but it's his cofounder Dustin Moskovitz who wrote an article that really stood out to me. The article he wrote on the platform Medium.com was called "Work Hard, Live Well." I'd highly recommend reading the article in its entirety, but I'll summarize it below for our purposes.

Dustin was speaking to a group of high school students, and was asked if he had any regrets or would do anything differently. He gave an unexpected answer: he would've slept more, exercised more, and had a more balanced life.

But that would've taken away from his focus and leadership in growing Facebook, right?

"Actually," he wrote in the article, "I believe I would've been *more* effective: a better leader and a more focused employee ... In short, I would have had more energy and spent it in smarter ways...AND I would have been happier. That's why this is a true regret for me: I don't feel like I chose between two worthy outcomes. No, I made a foolish sacrifice on both sides."

Dustin went on to comment about the things we've already discussed: that we are able to achieve a higher output when we work fewer days and hours.

"The research is clear: beyond 40–50 hours per week, the marginal returns from additional work decrease rapidly and quickly become negative," he wrote. "We have also demonstrated that though you can get more output for a few weeks during 'crunch time' you still ultimately pay for it later when people inevitably need to recover. If you try to sustain crunch time for longer than that, you are merely creating the illusion of increased velocity."

This is exactly what we mean when use the term "burnout." And Dustin goes on to explain that this type of burnout and inefficiency is found in multiple ways. It's found in the number of hours worked in a day or week, or even in the number of consecutive minutes a person works before taking a break.

There are destructive consequences of any period where a person works too hard, for too long.

"*Rest matters,*" he wrote, and later followed up with, "These companies are both destroying the personal lives of their employees and getting nothing in return."

Similar to what I've found at Tower Paddle Boards, Dustin explained how his new company's productivity isn't hindered by a healthy work-life balance, but instead, *depends* on it.

His company has a culture built around avoiding burnout, and he believes it aligns perfectly with profit-maximizing objectives. "We get to encourage a healthy work-life balance in the cold, hard pursuit of profit," Dustin said. "We are maximizing our velocity and our happiness at the same time."

In the closing paragraph of his article, Dustin makes a powerful and bold statement to his entire industry: we need to stop this madness.

"As an industry, we are falling short of our potential," he wrote. "We could be accomplishing more, and we could be providing a better life for all of the people who work in technology. If you're going to devote the best years of your life to work, do so intentionally. You can do great things AND live your life well. You *can* have it all, and science says you should."

My Takeaways From Dustin's Insights

The reason I really love these thoughts from Dustin is because they fly in the face of the traditional mindset, and they're an honest reflection of what could've been done even better. Here's Dustin, creating one of the most powerful productivity tools of all time, Facebook. And Facebook was acting like the stereotypical programmer or hacker startup, by working long hours and working really smart people to death.

Until now, this has been the expectation, and it's been glorified in the movies and stories about great startups. As a result, talented people willfully enter into this scenario, where they're pulling all-nighters in these Red-Bull-fueled coding marathons, cranking out as much code as possible. But now, even at a time where Dustin could say it was all worth it, he's got the wisdom and self-awareness to say something different: that it was not the best way to go. It could've been accomplished faster and better if he'd approached it from a more balanced perspective.

Let me repeat that last piece: it could have been accomplished faster and better if he'd approached it from a more balanced perspective. He admits he made a "foolish sacrifice on both sides." His work suffered, and his quality of life suffered. Those are powerful statements from someone who has created something amazing that everybody assumes was so successful just because he outworked everyone else.

Dustin is saying that, from a personal perspective, if he would have thought differently about managing his energy and his team's energy, he could have been even *more* successful. Dustin is showing us the new reality, by looking into the not-so-distant past. He has stumbled onto the same thing that we have at my company.

These are powerful statements, because they create a direct collision with this leftover industrial mindset that we're all still trying to bury: the old idea that you work harder, work longer, and that's how you make more more money and create more output. The hustle. The defining of yourself by your job, or by your possessions. The glorification and holiness of the workplace.

Bullshit. It's all bullshit, the traditional mindset. Its time has passed, and if we don't all acknowledge that, we're going to get, well, the crisis we've now got. The 9.4 hours of wasted life, the burnout, the deficiencies in health and happiness.

One Powerful Statement From One Influential Musician

By now, I've given you every logical reason that we need to reduce the hours of the workday, but truly embracing the idea is not something I can do for you. It's got to come from within.

In 1979, the iconic Bob Marley wrote a song called "Redemption Song" that contains one of my favorite musical lyrics of all time. It's perfect in describing the decision that needs to be made now, by all of us:

"Emancipate yourselves from mental slavery; none but ourselves can free our minds."

This is the point we're at right now, in our working lives, and in our society. We're past the horrific reality of physical slavery, but we are still very much in the grips of mental slavery. We're mental slaves to these capitalistic ideas that the more money you make, and the harder you work, the happier you're going to be.

But look at your arms, and your legs. There are no chains on them. There's nobody forcing 25% of us to work more than 60 hours a week. There's nobody forcing us all to work 9.4 hours a day.

There's nobody forcing us to work these long days and nights, ruining our relationships and making our children among the unhappiest in the world. We've got all of these ills, from obesity to substance abuse, to excessive consumerism and materialism. We're working excessively for a $75,000 car, when a $5,000 car would work just fine.

We're enslaved with the wrong beliefs, and it starts in the workplace. We're prioritizing work and money and possessions, instead of our health and happiness and relationships.

It's time to emancipate ourselves from mental slavery.

None but ourselves can free our minds.

PART III

———

WHY THE FIVE-HOUR WORKDAY WORKS

Chapter Six

WHY EMPLOYEES WILL THRIVE

—

WHEN WE LOOKED AT IMPLEMENTING THE FIVE-HOUR WORKDAY at Tower, we really wanted to answer the question, "Is this truly better for every employee?" I consider myself an employee, as well as an owner. I have a business partner, Mark Cuban, and I'm essentially a working manager.

My salary for working at the company is only $60,000, and it's a bit constrained because I have an investor. So it's easy to see myself as an employee too, and look at the five-hour workday from that perspective.

The following are the benefits for company employees, as I see them and as my co-workers have seen them.

Every Day Is Like a Vacation Day (But Better)

When I envisioned coming into work every morning at 8:00 a.m., it stung a little bit, because that's a little earlier than I usually began my workday. But if I just pushed myself to get up a little earlier, I'd be off by 1:00 p.m., free to do whatever I wanted to.

This is actually how most of my vacation days go, I realized. I get up late, grab a late breakfast, and it's noon before I get anything done. These days would effectively give me the same free time as a vacation day, but this is better than vacation, because it never fucking ends!

It's a work week that's better than vacation, in my opinion.

It really changes how you look at work. When your workdays feel much more like your vacation days, you knock out a lot more in the morning. It's not looked at as work, really. It's just what you do in the morning, and then you have your life.

Remember my friend that introduced me to paddle surfing? He was also part of the college contingent that travelled with me through Australia for three months. His name is Matt Madeoy. He has a business in Seattle called Sound Cleaning that does commercial and residential cleaning. He has an army of sub-contractors that he arranges work for and generates leads online. It's a highly automated process, but there are a lot of logistics for him to personally handle. He makes a great living at it, but it's a full time job running this operation.

When I told him that we were moving Tower Paddle Boards to a five-hour workday last spring, he was intrigued to say the least. I just spoke with him a month ago and told him I was writing a book on it, and he said he actually did a little testing himself this past summer.

It wasn't intentional, but he has kids that were out of school for the summer and Matt took them camping on the Oregon coast for a week right during his busy season. There was one week where Matt was put in a situation where had to watch his kids every day that week, starting at noon. He was forced to finish all of his work for the day by noon, so he could take care of his kids.

He was really worried about it initially, and it was a challenge at first, but it all went fine in the end. So at the end of the week, he just stuck with the new and innovative way he'd approached his business operations. He started working at 7 a.m. and finished by noon. The first hour of his day was now totally uninterrupted, and he dealt with all the previous day's calls and emails in a batch process, finishing all of them before 8 a.m. Those same tasks used to take him all afternoon to complete, and now he was finishing them in one hour.

The funny thing he told me is that he actually had his best year ever, and sales and profitability were up significantly. He said he wasn't doing it intentionally, but was actually working about a five-hour day and things actually improved! A few times a month he'd have to work long days, but he had created a new compressed baseline for himself, very similar to what I did at my company.

He's still on this same schedule, and it's massively increased his quality of life.

Health Benefits

With an abundance of free time every afternoon, most people are going to fill their time with some form of recreation and exercise. It might be tennis, or riding a bike, or any number of things. Exercise is a *huge* gain to energy levels and productivity, not to mention the savings for businesses on their health insurance premiums if everyone in the office becomes healthier.

This would drive millions more people toward a healthier life. In the eight-hour workday (and especially the 9.4 hour workday), if you want to exercise consistently during the week, you've got to get out of bed at the ridiculous time of 5:30 a.m., or dig deep for more energy at 8:00 p.m., at the cost of everything else in your life (relationships, family time, rest, etc.).

Is it any wonder that our society has become physically sick and obese? Look at how hard the typical workday makes it, for a person to exercise consistently.

If you're off at 1:00 p.m. you could easily plan on exercising for an hour or more per day. This benefit alone would change the life of most employees, and have a multitude of benefits to workplace productivity.

This also lends well to the idea of cycling, to drive other aspects of health. Exercise could be the focus for part of the year, developing new skills for another part, strengthening relationships for another part.

Relationship Benefits

We have a real divorce problem in America, and I think our overworking contributes greatly to it. I was just traveling in South Africa this past year, and someone I talked with on a tour of the townships was shocked to learn that 6 in 10 marriages in America end in divorce. He thought I was joking with him. It's more like 1 in 20 in South Africa.

South Africa isn't a wealthy country. Its per capita income is roughly one twelfth of that of the United States. To me, within its townships, South Africa is a borderline third world. In the townships, there's 50 percent unemployment, poverty everywhere, and it's sad on the outside appearance. But their divorce rate is 5%, and their kids are happy. What gives?

They have *time*. The kids are running around playing with each other all day, and half of the country isn't working. The half that is working, isn't doing it for 10 hours a day.

In America, the parents are working too long, not spending enough time with each other and with their kids. Parents are trying to catch one or two of their kids' games in an entire season.

What happens if American parents were done with work at 1:00 p.m.? They can catch every game, every recital, every community event. They can have time for date night with their spouse. Hell, they could rush home and shag before the kids got home from school. Or maybe just have time to have a nice, normal, unrushed conversation over the dinner table. Time to watch a funny movie together, laugh together. Time to love each other.

I did my last class of MBA school in Barcelona, Spain. If you go to a country like Spain, where they have siestas in the afternoon and the entire country shuts down for a few hours every day, it's about quality of life. We've lost that in America, in this leftover Protestant work ethic and traditional mentality toward glorifying work.

Human beings are social beings. Our happiness emanates from socializing with each other, both at a community level and an individual relationship level. Our happiness doesn't come from possessions, work titles, or retirement account balances. Our happiness comes from experiences and from relationships (which are experiences themselves, really).

The more time you spend with people you like and love, the happier you're going to be. No human being on this planet can argue against that. And the five-hour workday gives you the ability to do just that, as well as repair and nurture relationships that have largely been put on the back-burner due to a lack of time and energy.

Personal Happiness Leads to Workplace Happiness

When a person becomes happier outside of work, they bring that into the office with them. I can't really quantify how this helps a business, but Vishen Lakhiani from Mindvalley said it best: "Happiness is the new productivity tool." I've found that to be true in myself, as well as everyone around me.

Any environment where a team is uniformly happy, that's a massively productive environment. It might not have been as noticeable in the era of factory work, but it's extremely obvious in the knowledge working world, where we're working with our minds.

If your mind is unhappy and you're dwelling on a bunch of bad stuff, you can't be productive while you're in that mindset. We've done things at Tower to drive a positive mindset in everyone, but the most effective generator of happiness is giving everyone their life back.

Better health, better relationships, and better families. That's where happiness comes from.

Other Important Benefits for Families

In addition to the happiness-generating effects of spending more time with your partner, spouse, or children, the five-hour workday solves another problem: childcare.

School-age children are done with school by 2:30 p.m., in most places. There's a huge gap of time between 2:30 p.m. and the time when parents get home from work. Using the average American work commute time of 25 minutes (each way), and applying our earlier statistics on average workday length, those parents will be home at:

- **5:25 p.m.** for the 50% of America working 40 hours a week or less. They need to cover three hours daily with childcare arrangements.
- **7:25 p.m. to 8:25 p.m.** for the 25% of America working 50 to 60 hours a week. They'll need five to six hours of childcare help.
- **8:25 p.m. to (who knows?)** for the 25% of America working more than 60 hours a week, they're going to need over *six hours of childcare.*

What a nightmare. Our current workday requires working parents to find (and pay for, in most cases) three to six hours of childcare *every day*. And in the above example you can see that 50% of working parents aren't seeing their children until 7:25 p.m. at the earliest!

Is it any wonder why our children our unhappy? Any wonder why their parents are unhappy?

In addition to the cost of childcare and the problem of not having quality time with children, there's also the problem of what the children (especially the teenagers) are doing during this critical gap of time. It's safe to say that this is the period of time when kids get into the most trouble and danger.

Now, what changes if one parent or both parents are off work by 1:00 p.m.?

The parents have a full-time job, a good salary, and a sense of purpose outside the family that are all healthy. But they can also have a healthy family. They don't have to choose one or the other anymore.

I think the five-hour workday is especially helpful to women who would otherwise exit the workforce. I believe this is the type of tradeoff that many mothers would take in a heartbeat, and it might help to bridge the ongoing gender gap and gender issues in corporate America.

It's quite likely that you know someone in America, either a father or a mother, who has exited the workforce because the cost of childcare is about the same as what they're being paid. We have millions of talented people out there who are untapped in our economy, who could be productively driving our country forward economically, and they're exiting the workforce because of the excessive workday.

The five-hour workday is a great solution, or at least a great contribution toward solving this problem. I think it's a win-win for everybody.

Killing The Silent Killers: Stress and Burnout

In the current situation where half the country of knowledge workers is working more than 50 hours a week, we've got a real problem with stress and burnout.

One of my buddies from college, he got a really stressful job dealing with large sums of money, on the floor of the stock market exchange. The average retirement age at his company was 32 years old, and they say it's because of money, but the real reason is that the stress was not sustainable. If they kept doing that job past 35, people would just die at work, because it was such a stressful job around the clock.

Obviously that's an extreme case of workplace stress and mortality, but at 9.4 hours per day, the rest of the American workforce is creeping into a similar situation (without the millions of dollars to retire on at age 32). Corporate management consultants, for example, are being pushed to work 70 to 80 hours a week, and we already talked about the startup culture mindset that is similar.

We're bending people too far, for too long, and they're breaking. It's draining society at large, with a host of social ills and health problems. Similar to the famous fable of the tortoise and the hare, we could all function much longer as workers, if we'd just go a bit slower and preserve some energy. We could be healthy and working past the age of 80 on a five-hour workday, instead of burning out and needing to retire to prevent working ourselves to death.

This is exactly what Ford envisioned as the solution to what was happening in the factories, where a high percentage of workers were dying or being critically injured on the job, and there was high turnover and burnout. Ford knew that this was not a successful way to run a long term business. He knew it'd be necessary to cut down the hours, to drive higher productivity, and reduce stress and burnout.

Today is no different, except in this sense: we're not dying in a horrific accident at work. We're dying a little bit, every day, from stress. It may not go down as a workplace fatality—instead, they'll call it heart disease, or cancer, or diabetes, or any number of things that wouldn't happen with a shorter workday—but the truth is, it is work that is killing us by manifesting this stress on our minds and our bodies.

Lifelong Learning

Education and learning are definitely a commonly pursued interest of today's most talented knowledge workers, and lifelong learning is becoming an important survival skill as well.

The world is moving so fast. What we did two years ago is already outdated, and it's possible that what we're doing today is going to be outdated within a month or two. Lifelong learning is a necessity now.

Let's take an example of someone who has an undergraduate degree and wants to pursue a graduate degree in a new skillset. Right now there are Executive MBA programs that are one or two weekends a month, but people are exhausted by it with the typical workday.

When you're only working five hours a day, however, you could go to college full-time. You obviously wouldn't want to do that for your entire life, or you're going to run into the same type of burnout we've discussed. But for short sprints and cycles in life, you could definitely do that.

Formal degrees and colleges aside, all of the successful entrepreneurs and employees I know are building education and learning into their schedules. And guess who else benefits from employees becoming more talented? The business they work for.

This is how companies will gain a competitive advantage in this economy, by allowing time for their employees to learn. There's a lot of reading involved, and colleges and formal degrees aren't fast enough to keep up with the most recent innovations. You've got to constantly be learning, to stay competitive.

Side Gigs

Many fearful employers will look at the five-hour workday and are terrified that their employees are going to do side gigs, or work on their escape from your company. If you're one of those fearful employers, let me cut to the chase: your most talented employees are going to do that anyway.

Right now, just look at the typical career path and expectations of a talented knowledge worker. A recent report on Forbes.com revealed that 91% of workers born between 1977 and 1997 expect to stay at each of their companies for less than three years.

The most upwardly-mobile and talented knowledge workers move even faster. If you look at the typical startup executive's background on LinkedIn, many of them have changed companies every 6-12 months.

It's a different world, and nobody is planning on working for the same company forever.

The days of employees believing that a company will take care of them? Those days are over. Why? There are no pensions. There are few benefits that carry any weight. There is no college-style tenure, or protection from being laid off at any point.

Why are companies are still under the delusion that employees should be loyal forever, for their mediocre paychecks, decreasing benefits, ridiculously low vacation days, and—worst of all—their downright wasteful and excessive 9.4 hour workday?

Of course the most talented employees are plotting their escape. The more you try to stop it, the faster it will happen. But what would happen if you didn't fight this trend? What would happen if you actually *supported* your talented employees and their interests to do side gigs, or start companies of their own?

Well, let's look at that mindset and approach. First, because you know that this talented employee is likely only going to stay with your company for two or three years at most, you're not worried about retaining them for longer than that. You're just trying to attract the most talented, most productive contributors you can get, and create a culture that can do that consistently.

How can you attract those people? People who are entrepreneurial, creative, productive, energetic... and likely to leave? As one of those types of employees myself, I can tell you how: make it easy for them to do side gigs and plot their escape.

This is, of course, counter-intuitive to a strategy of retaining your top talent for as long as possible. But what you'll find is that many of these talented people will stay much longer than they would've otherwise, and some will never leave. But if you smother them and try to imprison them, 100% of them will leave.

The Other Benefit of Side Gigs: Money

Financially, when an employer makes it easy for a talented employee to work a side gig, and make extra money on the side, everyone wins. There's going to be less pressure on financial issues for both the employer and the employee.

The really bright people in this climate are going to get more than one source of income. I've heard the average millionaire has seven sources of income. They're going to do stuff on the side. So, if you want to get that type of talented entrepreneurial mind within your company (and you should!), then you've got to think about what that person would rather have: a 60-hour workweek, a 40-hour workweek, or a 20-hour workweek.

The answer is obvious, for that person. They want more *time*, not more money. Yet, many of them, because they're so talented, are getting big salaries and the 60+ hour workweek. Some are lucky and are getting a 40-hour workweek. None are being offered a 20-hour workweek, even though they're so talented that they're working 20 hours at most, inside their 40-60 hour workweek.

As an entrepreneurial or talented employee, having 50% less of a workday is worth more than being overpaid by 50% and working 60 hours. Having time for side gigs is a huge, huge bonus to them, because it's possible their side gig will earn them much more money than any salary they'd be paid. It also itches the creative desires to build things of their own, like Steve Jobs & Steve Wozniak tinkering with computers in their garage in 1975.

This is also a good thing for the American economy and job creation. Similar to the problem with exercise, where few people have the energy and drive to go to the gym at 5:30 a.m. or 9 p.m., we have the same problem with entrepreneurship. Few of America's most talented (and overworked) knowledge workers have the energy it takes to take on a second job (their side business) at 5:30 a.m. or 9:00 p.m., after a ridiculously long workday and likely cutting their sleep short too.

If you're limiting the amount of people that have the ability to create and test and run startups, you're not just limiting the entrepreneurial potential of one person, but you're limiting *an entire country*. Imagine the untapped potential of the most talented and entrepreneurial people you know. Imagine what they'd do if they were off work by 1:00 p.m. every day.

Yet Another Benefit of Side Gigs: Upgraded Skills

When employees work on side projects in their spare time, not only are they gathering more money for themselves, but they're also gathering more skills and knowledge. It's a huge benefit to me as an employee, to have time to learn new things on a consistent basis, and have the freedom to choose what those things are.

This becomes a massive benefit for the employer, too. Imagine this scenario: your company's best digital marketer drives traffic to your website by managing Facebook advertising and Instagram advertising. She has a side gig doing it for other companies too, and one of her companies sells auto parts. It turns out that auto parts are selling like wildfire on YouTube, so they ask her to advertise there.

She then spends a week learning how to create and manage

YouTube ads, and she's paid by her side gig client to do that setup. She gets great results for her client, and then one afternoon at her day job with your company, she realizes that YouTube would generate a ton of business for you too. So she gives it a shot, doesn't have to learn on the job on your dime, and sure enough, your sales are up 10% in a week.

Look at what happened here. She made extra money on the side, she trained herself, and it cost your company *zero money* and *zero company time*. She brought the skill to your company, used it, and generated a 10% increase in profits for you.

When you invest zero money and get an increase in sales, do you know what that ROI is?

It's *infinite*. It's the largest possible ROI you could ever achieve. And the five-hour workday, along with your support of side gigs, is what unlocked this possibility.

The Most Powerful Employee Benefit: Mutual Goodwill

If you'll trust employees to be productive within a five-hour workday, and trust them to have side gigs that don't interfere with their day job, and pay them fair wages, and give them their afternoons for exercise, relationships, and anything they wish to do, you'll get something in return that money cannot buy. You'll get a rare gift from your employees: goodwill.

This is an employee benefit too, because I actually believe that every employee wants to be loyal. Most companies simply give them no reason to be, and no path to be loyal.

Most companies treat their employees like garbage, quite frankly. A decent health insurance plan or 401k match doesn't make up for that. Health benefits and monetary bonuses and free lunches might reduce turnover, but they don't earn goodwill.

When you're an employee, and you love your company and your team, and your happy life that you job enables, you're loyal. You've got goodwill for that company. You'd feel guilty giving that company anything less than your best effort, every single day. You live and breathe this company, you're talking highly about it with your customers, and your friends, and anyone who will listen. That's what goodwill looks like.

When you're a company, the benefits of employee goodwill are obvious. But in America, most businesses don't understand these benefits, because they never come close to being the type of business that employees would be loyal to. Most companies rule with fear, instead of trust and love.

Most companies' structure is adversarial, and forces employees to have contempt and dissatisfaction. Most companies try to get employees to work as long as possible, and pay them as little as possible. Most companies do not share productivity gains fairly, or at all.

As a result, most employees try to work as little as possible during their long day, and get their Christmas shopping and personal emails and Facebook posts done while they're in the office. Most employees see productivity gains and don't tell their employer it's taking them less time to do their job.

And why should they tell the company? There's no goodwill in either direction. It's an adversarial relationship.

Trust me: employee goodwill is by far the most valuable asset a business can have. And employee goodwill is one of the best feelings an employee can have. I know this, because I experience it on a daily basis, thanks to our five-hour workday.

Becoming Superhuman

The objective of the five-hour workday is to make you more efficient. If you can learn to produce the same amount of output in five hours as what you did previously in eight hours, you have increased the value of your work. Once you've done that, you can keep optimizing your time and learn to do in five hours what most people do in two eight-hour days.

For my entrepreneurial peers, this is a prerequisite to being successful. You have to become super efficient and super productive to survive yourself, and then you have to do the same to will a fledgling startup business into existence. This is what I call learning to be superhuman, because once you learn to be massively productive, you don't just have to work five hours a day. You can work 15 hours and do a week's work in a day.

The objective of the five-hour workday is about lifestyle balance, but it's also about learning massive productivity as a team and how that makes your company very powerful. This is what the best entrepreneurs in the world are doing.

In 2013, I was invited to be a backup speaker at an event called MasterMindTalks, put on by my entrepreneurial friend Jayson Gaignard. They get over 4,000 entrepreneur applicants to attend this event, but only select about 100-150 to attend. About a dozen of these will give talks. It's a highly curated audience where everyone in the audience could just as easily be a speaker. The average business size of the audience members was around $8M.

The speakers that year were a pretty impressive lot. One was Tim Ferriss, author of the 4-Hour Work Week. Other notable speakers included: Guy Kawasaki, a brand ambassador of Apple in the early days as well as author of *The Art of the Start*; Mark Ecko, founder or Ecko Unlimited; James Altucher, a hedge fund manager, serial entrepreneur, and bestselling author; AJ Jacobs, Editor at Large for *Esquire*, and multiple New York Times bestselling author; Dani Reiss, the CEO of Canada Goose; Bruce Poon Tip, the CEO of G Adventures, a $100M adventure travel company; and on, and on. Really, too many impressive entrepreneurs to mention.

It was a three-day event and everyone would come back to the hotel bar and have cocktails until late in the evening after the day's talks. On the second night there, I popped out of the elevator on my way to the bar and ran into AJ Jacobs (who I was a complete stranger to at this point) and congratulated him on his talk, and said that I'd be voting for him in the "best talk" contest (the winner got $25,000 to give to their favorite charity, I think). Furthermore, I let him know how absolutely hilarious he was. He thanked me and invited me to drinks with a group that was heading out somewhere. How could I turn down that offer?

I make my way out to the hotel driveway and am quickly ushered into Mark Ecko's private car and off we go. Mark, who I am a complete stranger to at this point, is sitting upfront and we're all making small talk. I tell him about a joint acquaintance of ours who founded a production company called Smuggler that did a viral video for Ecko in 2007 called "Still Free." He knew my friend. They filmed a group of graffiti artists supposedly tagging Air Force One (they leased and painted a 747 to look like it) with the words "Still Free" (Ecko's tagline) and released it underground. It got 23 million views in the first 2 weeks, over 100 major broadcast news mentions, and at one point it was on CNN and the secret service didn't know whether Air Force One was tagged or not, so they got a little heat for it.

We arrive at the restaurant and it's a group of the speakers. I'm one of the last ones there and there's an empty seat next to Tim Ferriss. I'm a little star struck at this point. There are a number of brand names at this table. Tim is next to me, Mark Ecko is directly across the table from me, there are New York Times bestselling authors, big name VCs, etc. We all have drinks until like 3:00 a.m., and Tim picks up the tab.

During the evening I'm trying not to be too much of a fanboy, but I'm telling Tim how his book really changed my life and how thankful I was. And here now I'm sitting next to him at this table of renowned entrepreneurs having drinks. I let him know I wouldn't be there without his book.

We chat about it and at one point he says something to the effect of some people misunderstanding the object of the book.

It's not about not working as little as possible, rather it's really about learning productivity. He certainly doesn't work only four hours a week. That wasn't his goal.

He wanted to become super productive, and you do that by subtraction to learn what's possible. I read somewhere later that he really just tries to do one major task a day, maybe it takes 2-3 hours. And he's absolutely killing it. He's written several best-selling books, done a TV show, speaks on occasion, and is an investor and advisor to Silicon Valley behemoths like FaceBook, Twitter, UBER, and Evernote.

By the end of the night, I'd made some new friends (and pretty connected ones at that). At one point, after a few cocktails to loosen me up, I was telling Mark Ecko about my plans to potentially extend my Tower brand into an apparel line, and why it could be like a surf brand, but on steroids—due to the demographics, reach, and variety of appeal.

It piqued his interest. He asked me to call him when I was ready to extend the brand. I literally said, "That's a very nice of you, but hey, I know we're just talking here. I'm nobody. How am I really going to get ahold of you?"

"Give me your phone," he said. So I gave it to him, and he put his number in there.

At the time of this writing, I haven't called him, because we're not there as a company yet. But I've opened the door. And that door was really opened by a common acquaintance, Patrick Milling Smith, who is the founder of Smuggler, the production company that did Ecko's viral "Still Free" video. Any guess where I met Patrick?

On my 3-month backpacking trip through Australia.

Patrick was a like-minded traveler from the UK. I think he was 19 at the time. He was on his own "gap year" adventure, probably while a lot of his buddies were racing into the workforce. I kept in touch with Patrick after our trip and crashed on his couch in London for a week after my grad school stint in Barcelona.

A few years after our travels, in 2002, Patrick founded Smuggler. It was a production company for music videos and TV spots, which is a highly competitive industry. Within just a few years, his company was producing Super Bowl commercials. He wasn't even 30 years old yet. They won the Palme d'Or at the Cannes Film Festival, and it's one of the highest awards you can get in the film industry. Patrick's company won it several times. They were being named the production company of the year by the leading industry journals. Did you see the retirement commercial for New York Yankees superstar Derek Jeter? That was done by Patrick's company.

He's gone on to extend his work into a feature film company, and his directors have earned numerous Academy Award nominations. He's also produced Broadway plays. Their first play out the gate, called "Once," won 11 Tony Awards. And now Patrick is off on a new venture, a virtual reality production company called Vrse.works.

The reason I'm telling you about Patrick and his far-reaching accomplishments is that this is exactly the type of person who is thriving in today's knowledge worker world. These are the kids who were backpacking around the world while most people were in college, or racing to work like slaves in the corporate world, on a path to be the black sheep in our work-obsessed world. Patrick is a very hard worker, but he also understands and prioritizes his quality of life.

The "time-off," the living, and the adventures that most people see as distractions, are really the foundation of success in today's world, where creativity and knowledge work are so critical. I can point to all of my successes and trace them back to an experience that most people would scoff at as non-essential leisure.

My entrepreneurial drive? Go back to Australia. My poker

chip company? Playing a weekly poker game with buddies. My paddle board company? Going paddle boarding with my friend Matt at 5:30 a.m.

And if I ever extend Tower into the apparel category, those cocktails with new friends till 3 a.m. in the morning could be a critical piece, in retrospect. I believe that everything good comes from the off-time, the living.

Do you want to learn to be superhuman? Then figure out how to live, not just work. That's the fulfilling journey I'm trying to empower with the five-hour workday.

The Game Changer

Entrepreneurs like myself employ the five-hour workday to get what we have to do out of the way, in order to do what we want to do. That is often times more of what most people would call work. I call it a hobby. For entrepreneurs like Gary Vaynerchuk, it's definitely a hobby. For many of my entrepreneurial peers, it's the same. It's something we like, and it's something we're good at. This is how we positively impact the world. This is our contribution.

Not everyone is an entrepreneur whose hobby is more of the same work, and that's a good thing. For most people, work is only a thing they do to enable the rest of their lives and in many cases enable their real passion. For these people, the majority of our society, the five-hour workday is about creating productivity within a company, but it's just as much about freeing up time for productivity in other, much more important areas of your life.

There are many types of contributions that enhance society, and everyone has a different specialty, interest, talent, or passion. These other talents are what we are currently leaving on the table with our incessant focus on spending more and more time working.

Like a lot of people around the country, my mom worked

primarily to pay the bills. My parents were divorced for much of my childhood, so my mom took on the primary day-to-day role of raising three boys while working full-time. There was financial help from my father, of course, but it's still a formidable task raising three boys.

My mom didn't really have the luxury to pursue her passion in work. She just needed a job, so she started out at the bottom with a credit union, and over a period of about 30 years moved up and eventually managed one. She worked a regular eight-hour day and was usually home around 5:30 or 6:00 at night. Even with this schedule, she did a pretty good job raising my brothers and myself. Even though we grew up in a rural logging town, my eldest brother went on to get his Ph.D. from Stanford, all on scholarship. My middle brother went on to build a $10M company. And I really feel like we're all just really getting started.

My mother did a great job, but she had to make a lot of sacrifices. I wonder what she would have done if she only had to work a five-hour workday. As a mother and a rock to all those around her, I really wonder how much more she could have done and how much better her quality of life could have been if she had been given back her free time.

This is a big part of why I'm writing this book. World-class human beings like my mom deserve to be given their time back to do with as they wish. I bet you know more than a few people who deserve the same.

Growing up, I loved sports. Jerry Smoot was one of my little league coaches. His son was two grades below me. He coached me in baseball and basketball. I believe he worked for the local telephone company, not sure exactly what he did, but I did know he loved coaching and he loved helping out kids.

He coached hundreds of kids over the years, but he didn't just coach a practice and a weekend game. He researched tournaments we could go to in the U.S. and in Canada. He was going to the ends of the earth to find games for myself, my friends, and hundreds of kids to play.

He's well known and his contribution to little league sports in the Mount Baker community where I grew up is second to none. He had to have a pretty cool boss because he was everywhere coaching. I'm pretty sure he had a 9-5 job, but I can't imagine that was his focus as he was so good with kids. Jerry Smoot was a pretty special and pretty rare human being, but my guess is there are people like him in communities all over the U.S. and the world.

You probably know a few people like Jerry. Imagine how many more are out there that would love to help out kids in this manner, but can't because they're unwittingly tied to our 9.4 hour workday culture. Unleashing the true human potential of people like Jerry is a big part of what the five-hour workday is about.

I could list dozens more examples of exceptional people I know whose true gifts we aren't fully realizing in our current work-obsessed and materialistic culture. People who aren't given the free time to pursue their true passions, interests, and talents. Our society has lost touch with the reality that the work we do to make money is only a sliver of the real potential of humans to do great things in this world, and create an exceptional quality of life for themselves and those around them.

When we talk about lost productivity, this is what we should be really talking about. This is where the five-hour workday will be a game changer.

Chapter Seven

WHY COMPANIES WILL THRIVE

———

ONE OF THE TOUGHEST TRUTHS TO REMEMBER ON A DAILY BASIS is that, even though we're working part-time hours, this is not a part-time business. You're getting the same or higher output in fewer hours. It's full-time productivity. There is no loss to productivity, there are only gains.

What you're doing is creating an artificial time constraint that helps you find and unlock the productivity enhancements that new technologies have brought about. It's there in your company already, or it's out there waiting for you to find it and use it. When you create the time constraint, your employees finally have a reason to use the productivity tools you've got, or find new ones, or create new ones.

The Resulting Competitive Advantage

Now that the constraint is driving every employee to figure out cutting-edge solutions and productivity enhancements, you're starting to give your competitors a nice old-fashioned butt-kicking. You're using new technologies they're not using yet, you're getting PR from your workday culture, you're getting employee goodwill. You're gaining a huge competitive advantage.

Your Type A employees suddenly have taught themselves to be far more productive by using constraints, and they're really just looking at the five-hour workday as what it is, a baseline. It's no different than with an eight-hour workday where some people just push harder than others. When these people are driving projects in the framework of a five-hour workday, sometimes they are still putting in 50 hour weeks at times when it's needed. It's more of a voluntary effort though, and one that they don't see as work, or they wouldn't be doing it.

Meanwhile, your competitors are trying to make small gains with their overworked staff. They're trying to legislate long hours and pressure their staff into it. They're dealing with lots of employee turnover, because there's no goodwill or loyalty. They're having to pay a million dollars for advertising, to get the customer traffic that you're getting for free, from all your media coverage. After all that, if enough money is left, they're paying expensive consultants to teach them the technologies that your employees are already using, and learned about for free.

You're spending a lot less money than your competition, getting results much faster, and the competitive advantage is small at first. But then it grows.

It grows because of your company's new habits and mindset. Now, your company is full of happy, energized, self-learning, loyal employees. Employees who are working 200% or 300% more effectively and quickly than industry averages.

Your competitive advantage over your competitors gets even larger, to the point where you're not even in the same class anymore. After a year of this, you're now light years ahead of your competition. You're getting their market share, and you're getting their best employees. You're destroying your competition.

And from 1:00 p.m. until sunset, you're doing all of that from *the beach.*

A Real Example of How Competitive Advantages Emerge

In our company's warehouse, we've got to mail out packages, and we've only got two people there to do it all. Before the five-hour workday was implemented, they were working a full eight-hour day and it seemed to take them all eight hours to successfully ship our increasing volume of packages.

Switching to a five-hour workday was especially scary for this department, because it's harder to imagine how the same amount of packages could get mailed out in three fewer hours. Especially as our company was quickly growing to $5 million in revenue, then $7.2 million, and trending toward $10 million soon.

What changes took place in our shipping and warehouse, when the five-hour workday was first implemented?

A year prior, we'd rolled out a productivity application called Ship Station but we weren't fully leveraging all it could do. We just didn't need it back then, but felt it was worth another look now. In shipping, there are a lot of processes between the initial order and the ending shipment. You get an order online, it needs printed out, the product needs to be found and packed, then labeled with the right label, then shipped, then tracking needs to be gathered from the mailing service (UPS, Fedex, etc) and input back into our e-commerce system so it can be emailed to our customer.

Many companies just do all of those processes by hand, and we were one of those companies when we had an eight-hour workday. But the time constraints of the five-hour workday forced us to reconsider the advanced features of this shipping application that could possibly automate some of our processes.

The team dedicated themselves to learning to use this new

software to full advantage. It worked. It saved at least two hours of the day immediately. Now, our shipping employees simply clicked one button to batch 10 orders at once, print all 10 labels, print postage, acquire the tracking info automatically, and integrate it with the e-commerce system. All of that happened with one click of a button, in the new shipping app.

We still had to pack the boxes from there. Even though we had that new system, we still weren't maximizing all of its features. One feature was a way you can go in and program that system with the exact weight and dimensions of every product you have, and it will recalculate in a way that sends out far fewer batches. So now we saved a little more time.

We still weren't comfortable though, and wanted to find more time savings, so we began to examine the warehouse itself. How productive was this warehouse design? There's this thing called "spaghetti string theory," where they basically follow everybody around having to walk to do their job, and the total length of all the processes are essentially strands of spaghetti, and you're trying to reduce the length of each string of spaghetti.

We did that, and completely reworked the warehouse design and processes. It saved a boatload of time, and we were now shipping all of our packages within the constraint of five hours, with time to spare.

For three years previous to that day, we'd had this same warehouse and these same capabilities the entire time, and didn't know it. We had no reason to try, and no time constraint. Now we know it, and we're finding more ways everyday to keep driving further time savings and productivity enhancements.

As a result, we continue to strengthen a competitive advantage in our industry: compared to our competitors, we're shipping faster to customers, and we're doing it with much less labor costs, postage costs, and packaging/box costs. So we're enjoying better margins, better product pricing, and happier customers.

You might be asking why couldn't we just have management examine the processes and optimize things and then let the employees enjoy those same time-saving benefits in an eight-hour workday framework? Well, I suppose you could do that, but we're a small, very lean, and very flat organization. We currently have seven people and we expect to do $10 million in revenue this year.

In organizations like ours, you need every person on your team to act like an efficiency consultant. In small companies, they need to do this for themselves and their own tasks, on a continuous basis. That's what the time constraint forces upon them, for their own benefit, which is very visible when they walk out the door at 1:00 p.m. and go enjoy their life.

What If Employees Are Scared That Technology Will Replace Them?

There's a huge fear of technology right now, from the viewpoint of workers. They're afraid that they're going to be replaced by robots. And in some industries, they're right.

But in most knowledge working industries, technology is not going to replace them anytime soon. What we've found is that the real power of technology is when you blend it with human power. The wrong move is to save human time by automating with a telephone tree. The right move is to answer the phone with real humans, but use a website and FAQs and helpful You-Tube clips made by that same customer experience person to let people go online and find help, and to use that same person who answers the phone to also leverage live chat and email with copy-and-paste responses to typical questions.

The big win is using the best of the human touch, massively leveraged by the power of technology. Do that and you will separate yourself from companies that are using automation and technology to get further away from dealing with customers.

Employees still have that fear though, so that fear needs to be mitigated, if you're going to get your employees to trust and embrace today's new technologies, and look for more new technologies in the future.

When I came out graduate school in 1999, I saw a lot of companies go out of business because employees were afraid to use new technologies that might replace them. And as a result, the technology didn't replace the individuals directly, but it put their companies out of business altogether. By avoiding these technologies, their fears became a reality, and they lost their jobs in a way they didn't expect.

I was working in a radiology portal, which was a news, education, and information website and community, in 1999 when an online-only company was rare. We were trying to get traditional powerhouse companies to advertise on our site, and these were big brands like General Electric, Siemens, and Phillips.

Online advertising in 1999 was a very new type of advertising, very different from what these brands had done up to that point. To the 50+ year old marketing employees who were at the top of their careers, this was scary and threatening to everything they knew and understood. They were the decision makers we needed to sell, but they were all very resistant, despite the fact that we could *prove* how much more business they'd get from the new online advertising technologies.

Initially, we were spending $30,000 per month to buy banner ads that would show up when a keyword was searched in a search engine, and we were generating tons of traffic and business building our audience. Then, pay-per-click marketing came around with a site called GoTo.com that syndicated their results to all the major search engines and it was amazing. We could get qualified prospects to click through to our site, and it was costing us as low as *one cent* per click on some terms and even the most expensive terms were like $0.10 to $0.25.

Our costs went from $30,000 a month to $1,000 a month overnight, and we got about 10 times the traffic we'd been getting before. Talk about 10x advances! I was the new guy at the company, and I'm the one who found this capability. I wasn't afraid of new technologies. I was just the opposite, actually: I felt that this was my way to get to the top of the marketing industry, by leveraging the new technologies that everyone else was afraid of.

I was right. We reduced our cost by 95% and increased our traffic by tenfold, overnight. We were generating traffic for pennies, and selling sponsorships to the traditional radiology companies for hundreds of thousands of dollars, which was still a fantastic bargain for them as they were selling multi-million pieces of equipment. So these big brands would soon follow our lead, right? Or at least buy a lot of advertising from us?

Wrong. We had to painstakingly sell them something that was a no brainer for them. Our competitors and the big industry players didn't start using these new technologies en masse for about *six years*. Google didn't even launch its pay-per-click service until two years after we were using this. And by six years later, the latecomers missed out on the majority of the windfall of this new advertising medium, and the competitive advantage they could've enjoyed now as a result. We, on the other hand, built a dominant industry leader in our space in three years, from nothing. Why did this happen?

Fear. The big-brand decision makers were afraid of change, and afraid of the reality that everything they knew how to do was suddenly worthless, compared to the new technologies. Afraid of the truth.

Here's the truth: everything we're doing today will be done differently, very soon. Technologies will render our current processes and knowledge obsolete. You can count on this to be the truth.

But why fear the truth? Why not take advantage of knowing

this truth, and expect it to happen?

That's exactly what you must do, to stay in business today and tomorrow. You have to learn the new technologies that frighten everyone, and eliminate that fear so that you can leverage those technologies, before you get your ass kicked by competitors who are embracing the technologies.

This is the critically important benefit of shrinking your eight-hour day to five hours. You're killing the fear of being replaced, because you're creating an environment where everyone does need to be partially replaced (by three hours per day). But they all welcome this, because they're getting the same pay, keeping their job, and enjoying the benefits of this productivity gain by being done with work by 1:00 p.m. and off to the beach.

This reduces fear, and incentivizes productivity gains. Instead of throwing more man hours at problems, throw less and try to manage. Employees begin to use brainpower to solve problems. And in doing so, they realize that they're more valuable, and there's nothing to fear about the technologies. They're now talented and experienced at managing the technologies, and feel more job security than ever. And then comes goodwill.

From fear to confidence. From paranoia to goodwill. This is the magic created by the five-hour workday.

Financial Benefits to Companies: P&L Magic

This gets really interesting when you look at the financial benefits in a company's profit and loss statements. This is part of where Dan Price's $70,000 pay hike isn't as effective for most companies, because it's going to cost them more money in salaries. Not many small companies have an owner making $1,000,000 in salary, and willing to redistribute it, like Dan did.

That's why some restaurants were closing their doors in Seattle when they heard that the $15 minimum wage was going to be forced into effect. Those businesses were sending the message to their politicians that they cannot raise their labor costs, or it would put them out of business. And perhaps for some of them, that was actually true.

But with the five-hour workday, employees get a huge benefit worth more than money to them, and your costs don't budge. It helps drive happiness and fairness and productivity for employees, the same ways that a pay raise does, but there's no change in labor costs. Everyone makes the same amount of money (or more).

You're figuring out a way to pay your workers more per hour, and you do. But it costs the business nothing.

More Magic: For the Same Salary, Our Employees Got a Raise

When we went to the five-hour workday, I needed to come up with a way of explaining how everyone was actually going to earn more per hour, like how entrepreneurs look at their income. It's not just about the bottom line number, but the input that created that bottom line number. Maximize output, while minimizing input. The earnings per hour is what you are trying to optimize. Let's look at some numbers, and keep in mind that this dynamic holds true at any pay level.

Before we moved to a five-hour workday, the average entry level employee at Tower was making about $40,000. We almost exclusively hire people right out of college with no experience because we want them to be in learning mode and most everything we're asking them to do is cutting edge. Once they prove themselves, we move them up pretty quickly with a series of significant raises. A talented team member could climb from $40,000 to $60,000 or even more in the course of two years.

When we rolled out the five-hour workday, that changed two things: the working hours, and the per-hour earnings of employees. At the same time, we rolled out a profit sharing plan where we would take 5% of the profits, create a monthly bonus pool, and distribute that across the entire staff by merit. High performers would get a lot, some lacking performers might get nothing.

On average in it equated to nearly $8,000 per person in extra income per year, but our revenues are growing too. From the profit and loss perspective, it's less risky than a straight $8,000 raise because it's only paid if the company is making money. We were not actually raising our costs, we were just sharing some of those profits when have them.

Our profit-sharing effectively raised everybody's salary by $8,000 a year. Profit-sharing is one of the best ways to align company goals with employees' goals, and because of what happens when you go to the five-hour workday, this becomes even more powerful and valuable.

Per-Hour Earnings, Before and After

If you're working a 40-hour workweek and taking two weeks off every year, you're working approximately 2,000 hours. Truthfully, from our earlier statistics, we know that 50% of Americans are working at least 2,500 to 3,000 hours. But at Tower, our expectations were 40 hours a week, so I'm using 2,000 hours for our example here.

If we divide the $40,000 salary by 2,000 hours, we arrive at the earning rate of $20 per hour. So, $20 per hour was effectively our entry-level wage.

When we moved to the five-hour workday, the hours worked during the year went from 2,000 to 1,250, but pay didn't go down. In fact, annual pay when up slightly as we rolled out 5% profit sharing, which meant on average everyone got another $8,000 per year. So now, it's $48,000 divided by 1,250 hours which brings that employee to earnings of $38.40 per hour, overnight. And there is no increase in expenses to the company.

So as a company, you just increased employees' per-hour pay rate by a staggering 92%. You nearly doubled their earning rate, and it didn't cost you one penny.

Certain types of employees don't see the value in this, but you don't want those types in your company now. You want the entrepreneurial, productive type of person who values their time and yours. And that type of person absolutely values a per-hour raise from $20 to $38.40, as well as the extra time in their lives.

Doubling per-hour earnings while reducing the workday by three hours is empowering, and highly desirable by the types of talented knowledge workers that you want to attract to your company. But here's where it get even crazier: consider that 50% of the most talented workers out there are logging more than 50 hours per week. It's even more attractive to those people.

Here's how they view leaving their company to join mine:

- For the 25% of Americans working between 50 and 60 hours per week (2,500 to 3,000 hours a year), their per-hour earnings increase **100% to 140%.**
- For the 25% of Americans working over 60 hours per week (over 3,000 hours a year), their per-hour earnings increase **more than 140%.**

So for any entry level salary worker who is working more than 50 hours a week, for a $40,000 salary, that means they're making $13.33/hour (for the 60 hour workweek) or $16/hour (for the 50 hour workweek). When they look at a five-hour workday, they're looking at a new earning rate of $32 per hour.

The entry level worker sees a nice bump, moving from $13-$16/hour to their new $32/hour. But imagine how the overworked $100,000 worker feels, when they look at going to a company with a five-hour workday. That person would go from $33-$40 per hour, to $80 per hour.

When you're getting up into that high of an hourly wage, it has some really powerful benefits in employee retention.

The $100,000 worker is the type of talented person who is hard for companies to retain, because they can consult at a much higher hourly rate. $100 per hour isn't unreasonable, yet you are compensating them only $33-$40 per hour. And if they can build up enough clients on the side, then they can quit their high-paying day job, and put an end to their life-destroying 50-60 hour workweeks. You've probably seen this happen.

But with a five-hour workday, they're accomplishing the same thing: getting a high hourly rate, and ending the destructively long working hours. This is part of the reason that talented workers are going to stick around much longer in a five-hour workday. Hell, they can consult on side if they want to earn extra income, and you should be just fine with that because they'll be learning on someone else's dime, as I've already discussed.

Workday Reduction Should NOT be a Strategy to Avoid Giving Raises

To prevent the potential abuse of the five-hour workday, I want to make it very clear: reducing the workday should not be done to avoid giving raises. Wage freezes and a lack of incentives will ultimately ruin everything and sink your ship.

You're not doing what all the big box companies are doing, where they're just trying to shift all workers to part-time help with no benefits and no appreciation. Instead, you've got to look at this as if nothing but the working hours have changed. If you give raises every year, whether it's 3% or 20%, you want to continue on that path.

Believe me, when you announce the five-hour workday, employees are immediately going to think, "Wow! Okay, wait... what's the catch here? There's a catch, right?" And then in the break room, someone is going to grudgingly state the obvious fear that they're all thinking. "Bet we won't ever get a raise again," he'll say.

You don't want that to happen. Not just the reality of it, but the fear of it too. If not, you can say goodbye to any gains you might've gotten in productivity, loyalty, and goodwill.

It was critically important to me at ensuring that raises were delivered quickly, and I even timed the rollout by effectively giving everyone a huge raise in the form of the 5% profit sharing. We want everyone to have the same goals (productivity and profits), and reward them handsomely for innovating and enhancing those results. We want them to be more vested in their productivity and their company overall.

Recruiting Benefits: Winning the War For Top Talent

One of the biggest company benefits of the five-hour workday is that it becomes a very effective recruitment strategy.

When I started this business it was 2010, and our country was heading into an economic collapse. Unemployment was approaching 10%, and underemployment much higher. It was hard for new graduates (and everyone, really) to find a job. Hell, I looked for a job for 2-3 months with not one offer in early 2011 as I was trying to ramp up one company as the other one was dying.

As a result of this tough job market for job seekers, I was able to get energetic, talented, and productive people quite inexpensively. And that helps, as an early-stage startup. I wanted people in learning mode, and I needed them at the lowest cost possible. This was pre-Mark-Cuban, before I went on *Shark Tank*. But luckily, I was able to get really, really good people.

The economy gradually picked up steam, and that favors talented workers. It started to become a lot harder to attract the same level of talent, even though we had a lot going for us. We were on *Shark Tank*, got Mark Cuban as a partner, and we were growing like a rocket ship.

Despite all that, I was having a hard time attracting the best talent as easily I did just a few years prior. Then it happened: I lost one my best employees.

She was well-paid. At the time she quit she would have made the equivalent of $80,000 per year in compensation for the remaining six months of 2014. She started happily at $40,000 just 24 months prior. I thought she was surely still happy. I was shocked. As a business owner, I remember thinking, "What the hell is going on here? Why am I losing good people who are well paid? And why is it harder for me to attract other good people?"

I eventually realized that it was mostly due to the economy's improvement, and the high-paying startup opportunities being offered to talented workers. She was able to make even more than I could pay her, which really stunned me. She was maybe two years out of school, and she's leaving a job that's paying her $80,000 a year.

A year later, she quit that higher-paying job, and went out on her own. The skills she had learned while working at my company and the next company, these skills she had acquired in just a few short years were so valuable now that she had a path to work for anyone she wanted, or more importantly work for herself. And that's what she did at 25 years of age.

That's what's currently happening today, all around us. The most talented knowledge workers, the ones who are being recruited by the Googles and Facebooks of the world, they're being paid extraordinary amounts of money and offered all kinds of perks. Stock options, free gourmet lunches, onsite massages, you name it. If my employee above had a tech background, not just a business education, those salary numbers would have been $200,000 or more, most likely.

This is war. A war for talented knowledge workers.

How am I supposed to compete with Google and Facebook for these talented workers? We're still a startup, and revenue is climbing toward $10 million annually, but we still need to keep our payroll expenses as low as possible, if we're going to survive and grow. I can't pay new graduates $100,000 salaries.

My solution was to be cool. I thought, "We're an action sports company, and there are some types of people who might want to work for us because of that. We're a startup, and it's an exciting time, so we could attract some entrepreneurial people by emphasizing that. But what else can I do, to win the war for top talent?"

I knew that company culture mattered a lot, to top talent. We make products that absolutely enhance people's lives. The best employees care about that. And we had a good company culture at the time, but I wanted to make it the best in San Diego. I wanted it to be so good that people couldn't wait to come into work every day.

I wanted to create an environment that felt more like family. Today, a culture like that is so rare that it attracts and retains nearly everyone. People don't leave these family-like company cultures to make another $10,000. But what else could attract talented knowledge workers?

I looked at what the big companies were doing for these talented workers, and analyzed: what are they giving them, and what are they missing?

That's really where this five-hour workday came from. This was something that wasn't being offered by my competitors, and something I knew that my ideal employee would value very highly. It would be the icing on the cake: a great company culture, an exciting time of growth, a cool product and brand, and a five-hour workday.

I thought of what I'd want, if I were 22 years old again. And I realized that the five-hour workday would be exactly what I'd want.

From a career standpoint, at 22 years old, I'd want to have a workday that allowed me plenty of time to keep learning. I'd want time to have my own creations and businesses on the side. And from a standpoint of enjoying my day job, I'd want all the fun things that Tower is now doing: company trips, weekly fun events, and an office full of fun and talented co-workers.

So when we rolled out the five-hour workday, we included all kinds of new things with it that would further boost our company culture. I made it very clear at that time: we are going to create the best company to work for in San Diego. We're going to create and live a company culture that is so amazing, that people around the country and the world will talk about us.

We want to get the smartest people in the world to join us. People who can pick any company they want, and can name their salary. We want to offer those people something much better than money. And we want to give them a reason to work here for a very long time.

So that's what we did. We offered good salaries, but there are companies that can pay much more than us. It was the work-life balance of the five-hour workday, that's what separates us. It's the thing that almost nobody else is offering right now. And that's worth much more than money, to the types of people I want to attract.

The Two New Types of Workers You'll Attract

We don't have to go any further than Craigslist, to find great people now. But after we went to the five-hour day, we realized that we're getting two new types of people: talented people who love the five-hour workday for the right reasons, and lazy people who just want to do as little as possible.

The five-hour workday attracts the best, and also the worst. As part of our application process at Tower, we ask people to do a three-minute YouTube video and send that in to us. We create a lot of media here, so this makes sense to test as a skill. It's also an efficiency thing for us, as we don't have time to waste time.

There were some hilarious submissions, to the point where I thought they might be some kind of joke. We started to get this new group of people who were basically just slobs, sitting on the couch and saying something like, "Oh man... dude... I'd love to only work five hours a day. That would be totally awesome."

So, we're now appealing to the lazy people as well as the ultra-high-performing people. I didn't anticipate that. It's a challenge, because sometimes the difference isn't immediately clear, and we obviously need to weed out the lazy people. But we've been able to do that so far, and we've attracted many of the talented people we were hoping to.

But there's another problem, unfortunately. And it's not a new one.

An Old Problem Resurfaces in Our Newest Talent

One very impressive and talented woman reached out to us, after she'd heard about our five-hour workday. She emailed us out of the blue, and I was really impressed by her LinkedIn profile. She was driving at least half of the revenue at her company which was one of the top performing in our city, and looked like a super-productive performer.

She came in for an interview, where I learned how terrible the company culture was at her current job. How they were working their talented people well over 60 hours a week, and it was high-pressure, high-stress, high-burnout. The owners took all the gains and profits. No company stock, no employee profit sharing. Sadly, this type of company is now a normal one in America.

This company positioned itself as having a great company culture, and like many companies, it was a complete façade. Inside it was a cutthroat, competitive, political, burned-out environment, which is toxic. That's why talented employees like her leave, in addition to the insanely long hours.

The interview went really well, and I felt she was a perfect fit. I was ready to hire her on the spot.

"What do you make now?" I asked her. "Right now, I'm getting $100,000 a year," she said.

I was startled by that, but also impressed. She was only three years out of school. I explained that we started everyone at $36,000 and it goes up quickly from there. That wasn't going to work for her, of course. So I'd said I could get her in at $55,000 total compensation (salary plus profit sharing) to start, and it'd still go up quickly from there as she proves herself.

I began to emphasize how much the five-hour workday changes your life, and all the benefits of the new lifestyle that becomes possible when you're off work every afternoon. Then, to diffuse the money concerns, I started putting numbers to it. The numbers make a compelling argument with someone like this, who was working over 60 hours a week.

I said, if you're working 60 hours a week, then your $100,000 in pay is actually just $33/hour. Here, at Tower, you'll start at $55,000, working 1,250 hours (instead of 3,000+ hours), and that means you'll be making $44/hour. That's a 33% *raise.*

I could make this same compelling pitch to half of America, because those numbers would work out for them too. The 50% of Americans who are working more than 50 hours a week, they're being lied to with numbers. They're being told they make $100,000 a year and they wrongly assume they're earning $50/hour. But that last part is a misnomer, most of them are working many more hours than 40/week.

And yet, like this talented woman, it's uncanny how many super-smart people can't understand this, or don't value it.

I continued. "Imagine, you come in here. I told you that if you're as good as you say you are—and I do believe you are as good as you say you are—then you're going to be up to $80,000 here really quickly. Probably within two years. And when that happens, you'll then be earning $64/hour, which is nearly *double* what you're making now."

"Your workweeks will be better than most people's vacation weeks. You'll no longer be at a toxic company, and you'll be going into a workplace and family that you love being part of. You're going to be happy and surrounded with amazing people. And you're going to be making more money per hour."

Done deal, right?

Wrong.

As I would later learn, after many other conversations with high-salary workers, this is a large mental leap for even the most intelligent people to make.

She told me that she's now got a lifestyle that she couldn't live, with a salary of only $55,000. And keep in mind, this is a single woman, maybe 24 years old, no children. And $55,000 for a five-hour workday isn't enough. And the $80,000 in fast raises weren't enough. She said no.

To me, it's a symptom of our rampant consumerism, and a sign that even our smartest people haven't yet been exposed to the Aussie Mindset. It's a sign that our country is still steeped in a cultural mindset that prioritizes possessions instead of experiences, and values material wealth above time and relationships.

Almost every talented person I talk to is attracted to the five-hour workday, but many of them are still blinded by a focus on their salaries. Mental slaves, as Bob Marley might say. It's hard to argue that they aren't in fact enslaving themselves. They give up their entire life, nearly all of their free time, for what? Stuff that doesn't make them happy.

You've got to value your time, and the life that you can lead with that time, if you're going to understand the benefits of the five-hour workday. Sadly, even our most talented people have never been exposed to those possibilities.

This young woman knew she was very unhappy. Enough so that she sought my company out. We weren't even hiring. And I showed her a near perfect solution and a path to a very happy life.

She couldn't make the leap.

Ask yourself: how much is your life worth?

The Silver Lining

It's frustrating to lose out on employees that could be a great fit based on salaries alone, but it's a very-very good sign that very talented people are contacting us in a totally unsolicited way, like that woman did.

At some point, we will be a $30 million company. And at that point, I can afford to start a very talented person at $80,000 a year. When that happens, everyone is going to say yes. It'll be a no-brainer. And we're going to be stealing the best talent from every company in this city.

I could find a way to pay the $80,000 salary now, but it would be a bad move for both company culture and our operational strategy. Culturally, I can't start bringing people in at $80,000 dollars a year when I just recently brought everybody else in at $36,000. That would be a bad thing for culture, and unfair.

Operationally, we're still reinvesting all of our profits in the company to build our inventory assets. We don't want to run out of stock, ever, because that would kill our momentum. We don't want to run out of money, because that just kills us all together. But once we've stocked up and as we get onto more and more stable financial ground, we can start to leverage our profitability and be more competitive upfront on salaries.

For now, we're just trying to be competitive with our company culture, by creating an enjoyable workplace and fun family-like atmosphere. And it's working. We're getting talented people who turned down $70,000 offers to start here at $40,000.

If we apply this great culture to the more mature company we're about to become, with more profits to invest in more great people, it's exponentially powerful. We'll be able to attract (and retain) the best talent in the world.

From Absenteeism to Dependability

After recruiting benefits to a company, I can't possibly overstate the importance of the five-hour workday when it comes to reducing absenteeism. Absenteeism is baked into most companies right now, but it doesn't need to be. It's a productivity-killer.

You have some absenteeism that's happening in small chunks, inside the office. It's an employee who isn't working. They're there, but they're not really there. They're taking care of all the things they don't have time to do outside their 40-60 hour work-weeks, and they're able to do it easily because of all the recent productivity gains that few owners notice.

So, they're doing their online shopping on the clock, they're checking Facebook, they're catching up on personal interests and friends.

The other absenteeism is the traditional sense of the word: when employees don't come to work, or need to leave early (flex-time, essentially). This means doctor's appointments, kid's appointments, dentist appointments, and all of those typical things.

When everyone is off by 1:00 p.m., all of the absenteeism goes away, inside and outside the office. There's no time to check Facebook, and no need to do online shopping when you've got so much time later to do that. All of the appointments in your life that cause you to miss work, those are all now scheduled in the afternoons. Even vacation time is less strained, since every day feels like a vacation.

Past The Benefits: How We Did It

The benefits to employees and employers alike are very clear. Next, I'll show you how we implemented the five-hour workday at Tower, and how you can implement it at your company.

PART IV

—

THE TOWER PADDLE BOARDS EXPERIMENT

Chapter Eight

THE FINAL INFLUENCES TOWARD MY LEAP OF FAITH

———

FROM MY CHILDHOOD FRIEND MASON, TO MY TRAVEL EXPERI-ences, to my work and entrepreneurial experiences, there have been plenty of influences in my life that brought me to believe in the quality of life that is enabled by the five-hour workday. I just needed a few powerful influences to inspire me to move forward, when it came time to take the leap of faith.

One of those influences helped me understand that today's most productive employees are very different than the produc-tive employees of past generations. Understanding how these talented people are different today, and why, would eventually help me understand how I could attract these game-changing contributors to my company.

Bill Gates: The Value of One Great Programmer

Bill Gates once made a statement that made me realize how valuable the most talented workers are, in the this new economy of knowledge work. "A great writer of software code," Gates said, "is worth 10,000 times the price of an average software writer."

Not two times more. Not ten times more. *Ten thousand times more.*

In the industrial revolution, workers were mostly equal. You could swap out one worker and put in another one, and there would be little difference to the workflow. We designed our entire education system and economy around this idea, that workers are replaceable and interchangeable.

Companies measured problems in "man hours," thinking for any given problem: how many man hours do we need to fix this problem, or perform this new task? But that's the wrong way to look at things, in this new world.

In the knowledge worker world, man hours aren't man hours. What Bill Gates is saying is that one brilliant programmer is worth 10,000 programmers. He proved it, too: Gates is one of those brilliant programmers himself, and that's why he achieved the work of thousands of people, in the early days of Microsoft.

The same story applies to Facebook founder Mark Zuckerberg. He created Facebook in a matter of weeks, from a dormitory room. This is something that would take a typical company years, and million-dollar budgets, and a team of people to accomplish. But one brilliant programmer did it in a dorm room.

That's the knowledge economy. There's no more "man hours." There are Zuckerbergs, and there's average people. There are people who can do 10,000 times more than average people, because today's technologies amplify and leverage the brain-power of the world's brightest minds.

In most knowledge working environments, people don't really understand this yet. But in every single office, there are people who do 2 or 3 times the work of the average worker there. It might not be obvious, because the talented people are telecommuting, or running a side business while they're at work, or any number of reasons. But they're there.

And what's even more exciting to me, upon understanding this, is that there are more Bill Gates and Mark Zuckerbergs out there. There are people who can propel my company to a level of achievement that I can't even imagine. That's why it's so important to do everything I can to attract these brilliant knowledge workers.

This is part of the reason that it's important to create an environment that respects their capabilities and is a good deal for them. You've got to figure that these people are eventually going to leave your company and create their own, and that's fine. If I get the next Bill Gates or Mark Zuckerberg on my team for two or three years, our company is going to be in a better position than if we'd gotten 100 average people to stay for 40 years.

They're going to leave the company eventually, and become consultants or lead their own companies. So just be okay with that. Create a work environment where it's okay for them to do side jobs and plan their escape. I think you'll find the same thing I've found: they'll appreciate that, and stick around for longer than they would have otherwise.

That's loyalty and goodwill, and for the super-talented knowledge workers, that might equate to two or three years of staying at your company. Maybe 50 years ago, you could hire that Albert Einstein of the time for your mega-corporation, pay him a high salary, and he'd stay for his entire career. Those days are over.

Today, smart companies are literally buying startups for millions to basically get the founders or the team, and lock them in for a few years of employment as part of the deal. It's called an "acquihire." That's the world we find ourselves in today, and the value of some select knowledge workers.

Talented People Understand This Is The Golden Age

As I've mentioned earlier, this is the golden age of entrepreneurship, and the talented workers and entrepreneurs realize it as much as anyone. When you're getting offers to work at high wages, and then learning of consultants and business owners who are earning even more, it's only a matter of time before you start thinking about doing that yourself.

The barriers to entry are low, in starting a business today. The transition is fast and easy. So if you want to employ the best and retain the best, you've got to have what works for them. At best, you could keep them for five years before they actually go off on their own.

The quote from Bill Gates really hammered it home. The best people are worth exponentially more than average now, and they know it.

It's the golden era of entrepreneurship. So we've got to cut a better deal for them.

Creating The Culture to Attract The Best

After we'd become the fastest growing company in San Diego, the important objective I wanted to achieve was to create the best company culture in San Diego. My mind was constantly devoted to thinking about how we could do that. We'd built a very good work culture, but I wanted to take things to the next level.

At the time, we were working the standard eight-hour day. After I'd appeared on *Shark Tank*, I'd been taking advantage of the influx of press and media coverage, by writing articles on entrepreneurial topics like workplace productivity and culture.

I was writing articles based on topics suggested to me by our content marketing agency, Influence & CO. Somebody on their team came up with the idea of the five-hour workday as a topic for me to write about. Their thinking was that I was probably only working five hours a day, given other things I'd written and talked about. So they suggested that as a topic for me to write about.

That became the impetus for all of this, because in order to write about it, I had to think about it much more deeply. It stretched my mind, and allowed me to see that this would be a possibility for all of us.

Talking the Talk

Writing articles and being a thought leader is one of my favorite parts of marketing. I've written many articles over the years, but the article I wrote about the five-hour workday was especially popular. Within days of being published, it was shared over 1,000 times online. It really struck a chord with people.

I wrote that leaders, and possibly everyone, should be working a five-hour workday. And I believed everything I wrote, but there was a catch: I wasn't working a five-hour workday, and my team at Tower certainly wasn't doing it either.

The act of writing this article forced me to imagine how a five-hour workday would work for a whole team—*my* whole team—and that was a very uncomfortable exercise for me.

Honestly, I wasn't sure when we'd ever be in a position to attempt such a thing. Just look at us: we're exploding with growth, we're so busy, and there's just no way we could get our work done in five hours a day.

A few weeks after I wrote that article, I was at a small private conference of entrepreneurs, when a business owner I really respected commented that he had read my article in *INC Magazine*. He told me that he loved the five-hour workday concept, and asked me how we're implementing it at Tower.

With a sense of shame, I had to tell him we don't actually do a five-hour workday at Tower. It was just an article I wrote to present to possibility of it all, and that I believed it would be possible in the future.

And it kept happening, all day. I continued to be asked this same question, with genuine interest, from forward-thinking business owners. Some thought it was a crazy concept, and some thought it was brilliant.

Either way, everyone remembered it, and would continue to ask me about it in the months after the conference. It resonated with people, it was memorable, and it was very easy to conceptualize.

Finding Our "Why"

Later that spring I was reading the book "What Great Brands Do" by Denise Lee Yohn, an author I'd met in San Diego. She'd studied commonalities of great brands, and made a solid road map for building a great brand of your own.

I loved the book and couldn't put it down. I finished it in a single day on the patio of my apartment at the beach, while the beach lifestyle was happening right in front of me. Hundreds of people out there playing in the sand, and out in the waves, and cruising the boardwalk in the middle of a weekday.

There were 7 brand building principles in the book of what great brands do:

1. They start inside (employ a brand-as-business mentality)
2. They don't sell products
3. They ignore trends
4. They don't chase customers
5. They DO sweat the small stuff
6. They commit and stay committed
7. They don't have to "give back" (what they produce enhances lives)

All seven principles were extremely insightful, but that first one—the idea of employing a brand-as-business mentality—really struck a chord with me. Why? Because here I was, working on my business, trying to learn our next steps. And as I was reading this book all day, it's right there in front of me. Everyone was out there enjoying the beach. Living.

Here we are, trying to create the world's best beach lifestyle brand at Tower. We're telling our followers and customers how our products will improve their lives, and we know this for ourselves, and believe it to be true for everyone. And yet, we work in an office all day, just a few short blocks from the beach. The beach where all of this living is happening, everyday, right outside our window.

We're telling customers to take life by the horns. To live more extraordinarily. To live differently. To play more. But were we really doing this ourselves?

Walking The Walk

My team and I are really active people, outside our 9-to-5 workdays. But really, work is consuming those entire days and most of the nights. Are we being truly authentic to our brand?

No. Or at least, not as much as we could be.

For a brand that tells people to live differently, we needed to be doing that ourselves. We needed to commit to the "brand-as-business" mentality. It needed to be a part of our company fabric. And living differently means working differently.

And at that moment, it came back again. The thought that simply would not go away. And like so many recurring hunches we have, there's a reason the best ideas don't go away. And now I could finally understand why the five-hour workday idea kept recurring to me.

The five-hour workday was the key to living differently. The key to working differently. It finally made complete sense now.

Working from 8: a.m. to 1:00 p.m., that certainly is working differently. But what it enabled, that was right here in front of me. These people are on the beach, at 3:30 p.m. on a Wednesday. That's what the five-hour workday would enable.

And that, my friend, is *living* differently.

A five-hour workday would be a bold statement, and a way to authentically lead by example. Leaving work at 1:00 p.m. every day would be an unavoidable daily reminder of the exact brand we aspired to be. We would be different than everyone else.

We'd be working to live, instead of living to work. So why couldn't we just do that? It's my company, I can do whatever the hell I want.

Validating and Experimenting

The next day, I was thinking further about how we could integrate our authenticity into our company culture, and ultimately into our brand and products. I remembered an outstanding TED talk called "Start With Why" by a best-selling author named Simon Sinek.

The premise of his talk is that people choose to do business with you and buy your products because of *why* you do what you do, not *what* you do. It starts with the *why*. He explained that we shouldn't focus on doing business with people who want the products we sell, but instead, we should focus on doing business with people who believe what we believe.

The reason is simple: if you make a connection like that, then you'll have a customer for life. And you'll also have a great brand and competitive advantage.

And similar to the "brand-as-business" concept, Sinek emphasized that what you do serves as proof of what you believe.

We'd invested a lot of time and money, talking about living differently, and talking about working differently. We created Tower Magazine (http://Tower.Life), a beach lifestyle magazine dedicated to spreading that belief and message.

But now, we needed to prove it with our actions. We needed

to walk the walk.

Secondly, we were going to need to become (and remain) very productive at work. We needed to accomplish our work in 3 fewer hours per day, and we needed to do it while remaining happy and positive and not stressed-out. I wondered to myself, "What's the fastest path toward increasing our productivity in a happy and stress-free way?"

Enter MindValley. The founder of this remarkable company, Vishen Lakhiani, coined a very memorable phrase: "Happiness is the new productivity tool." He'd built an amazing company culture around that notion, and an incredible level of productivity.

I borrowed many insights and tactics from Vishen's company culture at MindValley, and I finally felt ready. I had the final piece I needed to confidently begin our experiment with a five-hour workday, and it was time to take the leap of faith.

Chapter Nine

IMPLEMENTING THE FIVE-HOUR WORKDAY AT OUR COMPANY

A FEW DAYS LATER, I CALLED A COMPANY MEETING, WHERE I announced the following:

- We're moving to a five-hour workday, as an experiment, for the next three months.
- We're also rolling out a 5% profit sharing plan.
- Between the shorter workday, and the 5% profit sharing plan, each of your hourly rates of earning has now nearly doubled.
- We're shifting away from our focus on revenue growth. We've proven that we can grow quickly, and will continue to.
- Instead, we're now going to focus on having an amazing company culture. We're going to have things like team trips, weekly fun activities, a weekly "stoke report," and a daily gratitude blog. And everyone on the team would be involved in deciding on these.

- Our new goal is to be the most desired company to work for in San Diego, and to be nationally recognized for our company culture.
- This is our inflection point. Right now. This is crucially important. How we navigate this stage will determine if we can truly become the world's best beach lifestyle brand.

The following Monday we initiated the five-hour workday.

We changed the website to add a careers page to reflect this, and guess what happened the day we did that? We had our first $50,000 day of sales.

Over the following two weeks, it kept happening. We had five more of these crazy $50,000 days. June of 2015 was our largest sales month in the history of the company, and it wasn't even close to the previous record. It was June so our sales were peaking, but this was still all very remarkable. We completely blew away the old monthly revenue record, by over $600,000.

Was this coincidence? Did our customers appreciate our employee-focused company culture, and buy more from Tower as a result? Or were more sales driven by our happier and more productive team, internally?

We did over $1.4 million in revenue during our first month of implementing the five-hour workday. Remember the 5% profit share promise? I kept it, of course, and the first month's profit share total was $9,800.

I handed it to each of my employees as cash, to emphasize that this is real. This is actually happening.

Then we took the rest of the day off, and headed to the horse track for the Opening Day at Del Mar. We had a blast. It was obvious already, the transformation of our culture, and our lives.

We were different now. We were living our brand. We were *living*.

And we never looked back.

Living the Values: A Lesson From MindValley's Culture

Mindvalley was a great company to study and learn from, during that period when I wanted to learn how to build a great company culture. I looked at all the things they were doing for building a strong company culture, which they were very focused on doing.

As I mentioned before, the primary insight I gathered from them is that *happiness* is the new productivity tool. And I knew we would need all the productivity tools we could get, if the five-hour workday experiment was to be successful.

Mindvalley exhibited how to create happiness in their employees, by aligning employees' interests with your company's interests and objectives. You've got to get everyone together as a team, talk about your values, and list them out, and agree on them. Then you've got to focus on them, build processes around them, and live those values everyday.

So we did that at Tower. We came up with eight specific values that were important to all of us:

· Be positive
· Be hungry and driven
· Be authentic and compassionate
· Be fun loving and social
· Be open minded and think differently
· Be selfless and family/team-oriented
· Believe my body is my temple
· Be a transparent communicator

Now, if you try to copy these exact values for your company without going through the exercise we went through, it won't accomplish anything for you. Your company's values have got to come from within.

They've got to be your employees' unique values, and your company's unique values, and there's got to be agreement between the two. The glue that holds this together is the process of talking to each other, forging these values, and agreeing on them. You'll need buy-in and cohesiveness, if you want to build a great company culture.

We wanted to have something we could all find value in, toward living the life we wanted to live. That list of values covered the important ones. The second part—the tougher part where most companies fail—is to actually *live* those values and make them a priority in the workplace.

We did that, we still do, and we always will.

The Value of Fun

Building processes and activities around our value of "being fun-loving and social" has been very effective one for us, when it comes to generating happiness. We throw epic parties. We've got a young, hip crew who have tons of friends, so we invite all of them too.

We throw beach parties so often that it's just part of our company culture now. We've also got team trips. Part of the crew went to Bali for the first one (I had to cancel last minute because I slipped a disc in my neck at that entrepreneur's summer camp), and the next one was a ski trip to Park City, Utah during the Sundance Film Festival. The whole company and some significant others went on this one.

We created "Tower Tuesdays," a random fun activity that we'll do on Tuesday, which might be anything from a cooking class to a Segway tour. We'll rent a boat with a hot tub, or go ice skating, or paintball, or do pretty much anything that's fun.

These shared experiences are a blast, and they're valuable to employees. Work becomes less transactional, less of "I'm going to pay you this amount to go to work, and you're just a worker here." It becomes more like a family, when you've got a culture like the one we've got now. You start to care about everyone around you. You work hard and play hard, together. You're not going to let each other down.

Beyond The Fun: Our Other Values Are Just as Important

The other values we established have also become powerful sources of productivity and happiness. We've taken it seriously, to make it a daily practice of communicating transparently and efficiently. As a result, we don't have many business meetings. We just meet with whoever we need to meet with, informally.

We've built processes around the value of being team-oriented and selfless. We do a weekly "stoke report," which is essentially a gratitude list for great things that happened that week, and it highlights people's contributions as well as anything else that is important to them.

We lead off the meeting with, "What are you stoked about?" We're a surf company and the word "stoked" is part of our language, but if you're not familiar with that word, just substitute "excited and happy." So: what are you excited and happy about?

It's a chance for anyone or everyone to voice what went well in the past week in our business, but also what went well personally. And also, what people are looking forward to in the next few days, in our business or personally. This really helps everyone understand what we're all excited about, within the company and within their personal lives, and it's a chance to give every single person the recognition they deserve. This creates a higher level of understanding with those that we work with, that you usually wouldn't get.

If they did something exceptional and just killed it at work, it's the acceptable time to brag. And that's a great motivator, because you might find a time during the week when that's some extra motivation to do a task in a way that you'd be proud of.

We also do a daily gratitude log, and it's amazing how that impacts happiness and productivity. I'd learned about the concept of a "Five Minute Journal," from two entrepreneurs at a conference (Alex Ikonn and UJ Ramdas). Definitely Google that and check it out. We watered their process down a bit. The basic model we go with is that you take five minutes to start your day, and you write three things you're grateful for. That's it.

As simple as it sounds, it really changes the way your brain works, and alters your perspective on life. A recent study conducted by the University of California observed people who kept a gratitude journal for 10 weeks, and compared them to two other groups who kept no journal, or a journal of things that displeased them.

The difference after 10 weeks: the people who kept a gratitude journal were 25% happier, had less health problems, and exercised 1.5 hours more than the other people.

It makes sense that this would happen. Instead of focusing on the negative, you're learning to ask what you're grateful for. And in our company's daily gratitude log, sometimes it's a stretch and something small, and sometimes they're really big and important things. But the powerful piece is the process of going through the daily exercise, incorporating it into our work culture and personal habits.

Every day, we use the popular program Slack for our "daily gratitude," and everyone posts three things they're grateful for. Everyone sees everybody's three things, and it builds. When you see what everybody else is grateful for, it helps you realize what you're thankful for as well. When they post, it also reminds you to post.

And when you read all of these positive things, and write them yourself, it makes you happier. It creates a positive environment, and prevents negativity. It's a relatively simple thing that every company could do, and should.

The Bottom Line

By following the lead of Mindvalley, and building our values into the company culture, we're creating happiness in people that drives an unprecedented amount of productivity. It's important for knowledge workers. Our mental state drives our productivity.

If you're happy and healthy, you're going to be able to work better and faster.

Testing The Waters: Our Initial Three-Month Experiment

When we rolled out the five-hour workday, I realized how difficult and painful it might be for everyone, if this idea didn't work and we needed to go back to an eight-hour workday. That's the beauty of words like "experiment" and "test," they send a clear message that this might be temporary, if it doesn't work.

Even though summers are our busiest month, there's a lot going on in San Diego and you can really enjoy the summers here. So I thought this was a perfect opportunity to position this experiment as something other companies might call "summer hours."

The day I announced it, I explained that this would be a three-month test. I made it clear that, if it doesn't work out, we'd be rolling back to the regular eight-hour day and I didn't want to hear anybody bitching about it.

Part of this was driven by the fact that I was really nervous about this. I understood that this was a huge risk. I'm writing a book about it now, but at that moment, it was not an easy decision. It was a huge leap of faith for me.

We only had 8 or 9 employees at that time. This could be a massive disaster. We weren't just doing this in the office, but also our retail storefront and our warehouse. The idea of reducing hours in any storefront—retail or online—is terrifying to a business that depends on it.

What Happened During The Experiment, And What We Learned

Our online customer service hours would now only be operational from 8:00 a.m. to 1:00 p.m. Pacific Standard Time. What we realized very early on was that it didn't matter. For starters, those hours are 11:00 a.m. to 4:00 p.m. on the east coast, and that's a great window of time to have all hands on deck.

Then I started thinking about it: we sell paddle boards. We're selling beach lifestyle products too, things like sunglasses and surfboards and skateboards. We're not a corner convenience store that needs to be open 24 hours a day.

When people buy a paddle board, they're doing that every three years, on average. When that's the case, what the hell does it matter if our office hours are five hours a day or eight hours a day? It really has no significance, to the paddle board buyers. Our online store runs 24/7. We could return calls the next day, if we missed them.

At our factory store, they'd just find a way to get there during our open hours. Our warehouse, surf factory, and factory store operate out of the same building, and that building is separate from our main office. The warehouse, factory, and store have their own five-hour schedule, but we needed to modify those hours a bit, based on the needs of the business unit and the customers.

Since the earliest pickup we can get from UPS is 2:30 p.m., we chose to run that facility from 9:30 a.m. to 2:30 p.m., and that also works better for customers who want to come to the store. More importantly, it works better for all of our workers who love to surf, since the surf is much better in the mornings. And those guys love to surf.

The online store works 24 hours a day, that's where 98% percent of our revenue comes from. Condensing our retail store hours to just five hours a day was a huge mental leap, but when you look at the revenue numbers on it, who cares? Even if our retail revenues dip by 40 percent, I wouldn't care.

But you know what? They didn't dip. Instead, customers did what's becoming normal: they checked online to see what our hours were, and they came in within those hours. We effectively just batched our retail customers: we had the same amount of customers coming into the store, at a quicker clip.

Online, the exact same thing happened. We had the same amount of calls from customers, but in the newly shortened window. Customer service hours were clearly displayed on the website, and customers adjusted. People who call after hours get a return call from us the next morning, and it doesn't hurt our business one bit.

Reminding Everyone About Productivity

It was important for me to make expectations clear, and make it clear that this experiment was not an attempt to shift everyone to doing the work of a part-time job. We're shrinking the hours of the workday, I explained, for all of the reasons I've listed in this book.

I knew that if I didn't explain these expectations, and explain that we accomplish the same amount of work in five hours, then people were going to think, "Oh shit, we're going to part time. I'm going to need to go find a full-time job now, or another job to supplement my income, because we're never going to get raises working these hours."

I explained that nothing will change about pay structure, because I still expected everybody in the company to be exactly what I expected before: two to three times as productive as the average knowledge worker we're competing against. If you're not able to accomplish that productivity, you're going to be fired, because we're going to bring in people that will. But I believe this shorter workday is going to help you be more productive, and that's why we're experimenting.

Wages will be the same or greater, and raises will continue to be delivered as they were before. But I'm attempting to give you a better life, and give you your time back, in exchange for the enhanced productivity that I believe we're going to achieve. This is the way I'm bargaining with each of you.

I believe it's a great deal for all of us, and if you're not willing to focus on finding ways to save time and leverage technologies and processes toward greater individual productivity, then there's going to be a lot of people out there willing to take your place. This is a great deal, and it's not in lieu of raises. This is the opportunity of a lifetime.

That's how I explained it to everyone, to calm their fears and suspicions. And the beauty of everything I said is that it's 100% true. This is a fair, safe, and lucrative deal for everyone involved. We just have to focus on improving productivity consistently, for this experiment to work.

How The Experiment Affected Labor Costs and Payroll

I've mentioned it already, but it's important to reiterate: this doesn't cost the company a penny. Payroll and labor costs don't budge. And that's how I knew I needed to explain this experiment to my new business partner and investor, Mark Cuban.

In addition to payroll not going up and productivity not going down, I explained all the other new things we were about to inject into our company culture. I pitched it with every ounce of optimism I could, because I figured that Mark would be a little suspect of this experiment. I thought he might see it as all of us just trying to work less and make the same money. So I had to explain all the things I've explained thus far in the book. And I put it in as part of my regular weekly update, which also included being on pace for a record month.

His reply?

"Awesome. Love it."

Mark is very intelligent and marketing-savvy, and I was happy that he could see that this strategy fits perfectly for our brand, the type of productivity we wanted to generate, and the type of talented minds we wanted to attract to our company.

And it helps that throughout the experiment, I was able to keep sending him checks, and remained one his best-performing investments from *Shark Tank*. It's hard to argue with results.

When it comes to mitigating risks in the area of compensation, the five-hour workday really shines. Consider the aforementioned experiment of raising all salaries to $70,000, for instance. What happens if that experiment doesn't work? That's a huge risk, because it's really hard to give a person a $35,000 raise and then take it away.

Higher salaries are also a risk when it comes to your product pricing, because higher labor costs need to be covered in your margins. You're hoping that higher salaries make people more productive, and in many cases that will be true. But what happens when that short-term boost fades away, and people are accustomed to their $70,000 lifestyle?

I believe it's the time constraints of the shorter workday that drive the constant innovations toward productivity, and it takes mental rest and more time off to consistently achieve those innovations. Or as Ford put it so eloquently 100 years ago, "The pressure will bring better methods."

For no increase in expense, the five-hour workday is an experiment toward generating productivity, and I believe it's more effective than other ideas that involve more money. It's more effective at teaching everyone to be more productive.

A Powerful Ingredient: Making Everyone a Stakeholder

Another critically important ingredient to add into the recipe of productivity, especially for a five-hour workday, is to create a situation where employees are stakeholders who benefit from profits and productivity.

Stock options, to me, aren't nearly as valuable as profit sharing. At some of the larger and consistently-growing tech companies like Google and Facebook, stock options definitely have value for workers. But for most companies and workers, stock options rarely amount to much.

And how much impact does an employee have over a company's stock price, or exit valuation? More importantly for this discussion, how much impact does the employee *believe* they have? Because it's that belief that drives motivation.

Of these two scenarios, which do you think is more motivating to most people?

1. An employee who is offered 10,000 stock options for a startup that isn't even publicly traded yet, and may never be acquired or publicly traded. These options will make you rich, if we become a billion-dollar company. And by the way, it's going to be five years before this is even remotely possible, or before your options are fully vested and you can cash them in.
2. An employee who is offered a job at Tower Paddle Boards, where there's a growing company with a profit-sharing plan that averages $8,000 per year in bonuses to each employee, to start. And it could be more, because we're a small team and each person can push that needle higher.

I'd pick number two, and I believe it's better for everyone involved.

I chose number one in the past, as an employee, and I learned my lesson. I was offered thousands of stock options with a company, and it was eventually acquired for around $35 million. My thousands of options were worth a paltry $3,000. I realized that stock options are a somewhat deceptive recruiting tool, and the options are usually worth much less than they're perceived to be worth... unless you company is a moonshot that turns into a billion-dollar unicorn. Frankly, your odds would be better to play the lottery.

But if a company has a proven history of awarding $8,000 a year, with the probability of it going up further the next year, and a chance for me to personally impact the amount I receive? Now we're talking. That's a bonus that I have more control over earning.

What's The Best Way To Structure a Profit Sharing Plan?

The way we do profit sharing has multiple benefits for both employees and owners. Mark Cuban really guided me on this. He gave me ideas and insights from his past and current companies.

In one of his earlier businesses, if it was a good month, he'd go around and just hand out $100 bills in a completely random fashion. He'd say, "Hey, you're doing a great job, here's a couple hundred bucks." It was unpredictable, and nobody ever knew bonuses were coming, until they did.

At his suggestion, that's basically how I'd done it in the history of my company. But when it came time to roll out the more formal profit sharing plan, we had to figure out a better way. So it was time to look at what others were doing, and what they weren't, and find our sweet spot.

Many companies that utilize profit sharing, they simply give everybody an equal portion of the total profit sharing amount. Employees can see the bonus coming, and expect it. The problem I see with this is that the bonus just becomes assumed as part of your salary. If you don't get that bonus, it feels like the company just cheated you.

But from an employer perspective, if you didn't make money, there's simply no money to share. Sometimes there are years where companies don't make money, there are years where companies lose money. You need to structure profit sharing in a way that shares responsibility for losses, and motivates each individual to drive productivity and profits.

It's dangerous to do profit sharing in a way that doesn't truly incentivize individual productivity, where employees think they'll get their share simply by being employed there. You might as well just give everybody a salary raise, if that's the case.

How We Do Our Profit Sharing Plan

Initially we did a monthly distribution of our profit sharing amount (we've since switched to quarterly so the big bonuses make more of an impact), with a pool of total money that is 5% of our monthly profits. The money isn't distributed evenly, however. We've tied it to productivity measures, and peer reviews.

Every employee rates every other employee that they work with, giving them a score of 0, 1, 2, or 3. Zero is for people just doing their job, nothing special. Three is for extraordinary effort and productivity.

The purpose of this is to make everybody think like the co-owners that we effectively are. Evaluate others based on productivity, while having an incentive to be productive themselves.

Those rankings come into me, and nobody knows how other people are ranking them. I'll then take that data and make my own subjective decisions, based on that. I won't go purely off of what other people are rating people, but I'll use that as a heavy influencer. That data gives you an insight into how people are working together and who's really driving apart a group's productivity.

We'll then take the month's productivity bonus, say it's $10,000, and we'll give two people $3,000 each, a bunch of people would get $500, and a few would get nothing. That's how we wanted it to be. We wanted it to be this very Draconian bonus system that gives people a real incentive to be extraordinarily productive and a great team player.

This system offers another critically important component, when it comes to attracting the talented employee who can do the work of 10,000 others. Those people are very driven by performance, and being rewarded with a heavy share of that bonus pool recognizes that financially as well as emotionally.

Ideally everybody consistently achieves peer ratings of 3, and you start firing off the people who are consistently given a 0. That's an important part of this five-hour workday, because if you don't have a continuous incentive that drives further improvements in productivity, everybody is just going to settle into their old habits from the eight-hour workday. Back to online shopping and Facebook and fantasy football, instead of giving 100%.

For the five-hour workday to work, you've got to teach the mindset of productivity, and give them the right tools to achieve it. You've got to set clear expectations and back it up with a good reward system, like this profit-sharing plan. And then you're got to start firing the low-end performers and recruiting the high-end people. You've got to have all those parts, for this to work in the mid-term and long-term.

Hiring and Firing: Acting on What You'll Learn

The five-hour workday experiment will bring forward many new insights, when it comes to which employees you should retain and which you shouldn't. And you've got to fire your least productive employees to make room for the highly productive employees who want to work for you, after they hear about your five-hour workday.

Remember, one of the most powerful benefits of the five-hour workday is that it helps you retain your best talent, and recruit more of the best talent. We're very early into this experiment ourselves, and still measuring what we're doing. But I already know that there are a few employees in my company who are not going to last much longer, if they continue on the unproductive path they're on.

They'll be fired and we'll bring in better talent, because I know that's what I've got to do in order to take full advantage of the recruiting and retention benefits of the five-hour workday. Employees are getting a great deal, and the company needs to get their half of the deal: greater profits and productivity. And there will be plenty of talented people ready and willing to help the company achieve that. You need to get rid of the people that this doesn't work for.

The five-hour workday is not going to work for every employee. It's going to show you pretty quickly who is unwilling or incapable of being productive in the innovative way that we're looking for. You've got to be serious about weeding out those people.

The Evolution of Our Company Culture

The many changes we made toward improving our company culture really started to blend together in an impactful way. It worked pretty much how we'd hoped it would.

From day one at Tower Paddle Boards, long before we moved to the five-hour workday, we wanted happy workers, and part of that was getting rid of the unhappy ones (or the ones who were driving unhappiness in everyone around them).

We had some people in the company who were negative, and we fired them. We came to the conclusion that we'd rather have a hole in our company, than have an asshole in our company. So we fixed that piece first.

After that, we could focus on making our remaining people happier. All of the new programs and values and processes were designed to reinforce these values. We wanted everyone working well together. We wanted them grading each other, trying to help each other and make a good impression on each other (instead of just trying to impress the boss). We wanted everyone to became empowered and accountable.

In addition to the profit sharing, we rolled out the daily gratitude log, the company parties and trips, and the mindset of the five-hour workday. People started to know their co-workers on a much deeper level, which was really healthy for the company. Everybody started to evolve into a happier and more productive mindset.

The Importance of Positioning This as a Baseline, Not a Maximum

Overall, our entire team was pretty stoked about the five-hour workdays, especially with the newly enhanced company culture and profit-sharing plan. I think everybody was pretty happy.

At that point, knowing that we needed to continue to be a high-performing company, it felt important to communicate that the five-hour workday was simply a new baseline, not a maximum number of hours. I started to notice that different people have different assumptions about this newly-shortened workday, and it needed to be addressed.

It is unavoidable that many people will continue to work 12 hour days. I'm one of those people, sometimes. But it's also what happens when your work is aligned with your personal interests.

For example, we have a filmmaker on staff, and the nature of that job contains a lot of filming and editing. When he recently went on vacation to Bali, he filmed a lot of material to use at Tower. I didn't ask him to do it, he doesn't feel pressure to do it, but he *wants* to. It's his passion.

Other people we have in our company, they're passionate about their work and our brand as well. The people in the warehouse are also in the same building as our surfboard factory, and they're sometimes in there on Friday nights at 11:00 p.m., posting pictures of a cool new surfboard they're making.

On the other hand, some people look at the five-hour work-day and they stick to those hours. They enjoy what they're doing too, but they're taking full advantage of the productivity-generating free time. They're productive and get their work done, and join in for our company activities, and are more than willing to stay extra hours if their team needs them to. These people are fine, no problem here.

The problem comes from people who likely forged their mindset in a work environment where they were paid hourly to simply show up. These are the people who come into an eight-hour job at exactly 8:00 a.m. and leave exactly at 5:00 p.m., so they just interpret the shorter workday as meaning, "I'll always be out of here by 1:00 p.m."

We don't have many of those people at Tower, and soon we'll have none of them. If anyone exhibits this type of mindset, I explain that the five-hour workday is only a new baseline of required hours. It's not a new baseline of reduced *expectations.*

There were points during this experiment where I sent company-wide emails, saying in so many words, "Look, I'm probably going to fire people who aren't producing, because we've now got tons of talented and productive people knocking on our door. Our new working hours are just a new baseline of hours, not a baseline of lower production and output."

"Just as before, if you had a 40-hour workweek and you weren't producing, that's a big problem. If you were working exactly 40 hours and checking out at exactly 5:00 p.m., but you're a massive producer, that was perfectly fine. And if you're working long hours, and you're not necessarily producing as much as you could, but I can see that extra effort, you're fine as well. I just figure you'll get there."

"But one thing doesn't change: if you're not producing to your potential, and you're only working the minimum number of hours while you're under-producing, then you're gone."

This became one of the things I wish I could go back and do better from the beginning. I would be much more clear that there are going to be times when we've got something that necessitates us to grind late into the evening, just like the old days. Maybe it's an influx of orders around Christmas, or maybe we're on TV again and order volume explodes again.

There will be 60-hour weeks again, here and there. We still need maximum effort at all times. That hasn't changed.

A different way to explain it: you're going to get paid a salary for working here for a year, and that salary is not tied to hours in any way. At some points of the year, you're going to have to hustle. Sometimes we have to grind really hard, and sometimes we're going to be skating along smoothly. But there are still going to be times we'll all be working 60-hour weeks, maybe even for a couple weeks at a time.

Knowledge workers who come from a salaried background, for the most part, already understand this. They've already worked in that environment, although it was more like moving from a 9.4-hour workday to a 16-hour workday during emergencies and crunches.

The knowledge workers already get it. It's the staff who are accustomed to an hourly pay rate that you've got to be careful with. But assuming you're clear about this piece, then the magic of the five-hour workday can gradually begin to forge great habits across the company.

No Such Thing as Overnight Success

Over the course of time, employees really start to become more productive, but it's a gradual process. The pace has simply picked up, and there's less waste and screwing around. It's a learning curve that you've got to experience though, to know where the waste was occurring.

What's happened with the 9.4-hour workday is that people

have been trained to be lazy, in a similarly gradual way. It's about bad habits, and you've got to break those 9.4-hour workday habits. Even personally myself, I struggle with some of those old habits. It's a problem for entrepreneurs and owners as much as anyone, because they settle back into working 9.4 hours because that's what you think you're supposed to work.

You go in at 8:00 a.m. and come out at 5:00 p.m., and sometimes you have to wonder to yourself: "Did I accomplish anything important today? What the hell am I doing here? I'm wasting my own time." Then you adjust it, and adjust again, and again. Then, after four of five years of these small improvements in productivity, you've got it dialed in. Trust me, I've been at this entrepreneurial thing for over 12 years at this point, and it took me constant tweaking and adjusting. You can expect this of your team as well. It will be a process.

Expecting overnight success is a recipe for disaster. People aren't going to immediately be 2-3 times more productive solely because of the new time constraints of the five-hour workday. It's a learning process as well. I've noticed that some types of people are picking it up better than others. I'm realizing that some types of people may never pick it up, and I know I may have to get rid of those people.

PART V

THE FUTURE

OF WORK

Chapter Ten

HOW WE MIGHT LIVE AND WORK, SOON

IN YOUR JOURNEY TOWARD UNDERSTANDING WHY THE FIVE-hour workday is a great tool for today as well as tomorrow, let's take a quick look into the possibilities ahead in the near future.

Manufacturing New Levels of Productivity

The American workforce, if given a better deal, will become massively more productive. The fact that technology has driven massive gains in our ability to produce more, but our corporations and owners have not yet changed the standard eight-hour workday, has led to the creation of a lazy workforce.

Talented workers know that they don't have to work hard or fast anymore, and it's made our country soft, and susceptible to being overcome by countries of workers who are happier and more productive.

By adjusting the expected productivity rate of the work environment on a mass scale, our entire working class will gradually learn to become more efficient and innovative. They won't be able to throw hours at things and get by. They won't be able to dodge technology. It will effectively force them to leverage the advantages of modern technology to work faster.

Workers will still have the same 24 hours a day to live, but only five of those hours will be focused on work, and they'll be more productive as a result. If they choose to spend another five hours a day doing working to make additional income, they could do that too, but the productivity gains within their five hours alone will likely lead to at least a doubling of each person's daily output.

When this happens throughout an entire society, it would effectively double the output and productivity of the nation. Just as some people today are doing three times the work of everyone around them, we'd all be pushed to emulate these highly productive workers, and we'd all have a fair deal and incentive to do it.

Increasing Lifestyle Consumption

The more people work, the less they have free time to purchase goods and services. When Henry Ford moved to a five-day workweek, an eight-hour day, and double wages, part of his logic was that he didn't want to make cars for just the wealthy people. There simply weren't enough of them. If the working class suddenly had more money and more time, they would consume more.

The productivity advances of the assembly line empowered Ford's change, and he simply took the next logical step. And Ford got what he'd hoped for: a universal five-day workweek, eight-hour day, and livable wages across the nation. That's when the consumer economy was created, and it was technology—tools for the body—that created it.

In the future, the same logic could follow. With more time off, people will have even more time to consume. But I'd argue that it's much more important that they will have an abundance of leisure time. Most people only have two or three hours of free time every night, and that's a generous estimate.

When people are off work every day at an earlier hour, they're going to have a better lifestyle, and consume it. Imagine how radically your life would change if you were done with work at 1:00 p.m. every afternoon? Your relationships, interests, education, health, and happiness are all going to improve. That will be the new type of consumption driven by the five-hour workday.

Decreasing Wasteful Practices

America is in a crisis of time starvation, and you can see it in the products and services we buy. Everything is disposable, and it's creating an unsustainable trend. I've heard that just the bags that Americans throw away in their garbage is more waste then most countries generate. Just the plastic bags themselves, not the garbage contained in them! We've convinced ourselves that we don't have time to do anything sustainably, but that tide will soon shift.

We're currently paying $5 to drive through Starbucks and save two minutes in the morning, instead of making coffee at home. We toss the cup in the garbage. It's a waste of money and natural resources. The same thing happens at lunch and at night, with cooking. Americans eat out often, many families just grab fast food from a drive through on the way home. And of course, we toss the plastic bag, the styrofoam carton, the unused plastic utensils, and more.

We're constantly on the run, because of our working hours. Our breakfast is a smoothie in a styrofoam cup. We'll happily pay $3 for 12 ounces of water, if it's in a bottle and we can grab it on the run. And now, the ocean is full of these bottles.

The examples are all around you, if you'll look for them. Examples of things we'd consume differently—and less expensively and less wastefully—if we simply had more time.

Increasing Societal Health

Eating healthy food and getting adequate exercise is a big part of living a healthy life. In our current time-starved culture, we make deadly trade-offs in both of these areas. We eat out way too much, we eat far too much processed, quick-to-make food. We eat way too much fast food.

It's literally killing us. A good chunk of the population doesn't even know how to cook anymore. And it's no surprise, working 9.4 hours on average. With long hours at desk jobs, as a nation we're not only too busy to cook healthy food, but we're also working sedentary jobs and becoming very inactive physically. Our free time is a couple of hours in the front of the TV because we're mentally exhausted from working all day, and we don't have much time or energy to do anything at that point.

This will change when you dramatically increase the chunk of free time people have each day. If you're off by 1:00 p.m., you've got a full day to fill, and it's likely that you're going to do something fun and active, and take time to eat in a more healthy and less wasteful way.

Improving Relationships

As I mentioned earlier, our children are unhealthy and unhappy. The wellbeing of American's children ranks 26th on a recent study of the well being of children in 29 advanced economies.

This is driven very heavily by our excessive working hours in America. Kids' parents aren't around. But with one or both parents getting off by 1:00 p.m., kids and parents could spend much more time together, building healthier relationships and greater happiness.

The divorce rate in America is high. Marital relationships are struggling. It's so bad that less and less people are even attempting to get married. Loneliness has become a crisis of its own, reaching record levels. People simply don't have enough free time to spend quality time with each other, enjoying leisure activities and life with other people. Technology can isolate us a bit, and we're still working too much.

How Healthier Relationships Replace Unhealthy Addictions

In 1971, in the height of the Vietnam War, two congressmen returned from Vietnam with horrifying news: 15% of our soldiers were addicted to heroin. One month later, President Richard Nixon declared a "war on drugs," which has been an ongoing disaster ever since. As a society, we have not addressed the true problem, despite the fact that the data has been right in front of us the entire time.

Various studies between 1970-1980 found that caged rats in laboratories confirmed our fear of these new drugs. The rats were choosing morphine-laced water over plain water, every single time, and becoming quite addicted to morphine. The scientific community, our government, and our entire society came to their collective conclusion: these drugs were irresistible and addictive to anyone who tried them.

But one guy had a different hunch. He was a Canadian Psychologist named Bruce Alexander, and he sensed that drug addiction might be driven by the user's environment, much more than the assumed addictiveness of the drug itself.

So, much like the five-hour workday experiment, he changed the rules of the game. He changed the rules and constraints that everyone assumed to be normal. The intense focus on the rats' behavior inside the cage, he thought, was looking past the thing that might actually be the problem: the cage itself.

And so he built "Rat Park." It was a beautiful area for the lab rats, 200 times larger than the average rat cage, and contained the elements of a normal, non-laboratory life. There was much more to do, more space to do it. Most importantly, there was a healthy and vibrant community of fellow rats to interact with, in Rat Park.

In 1981, Alexander released the results of his study: the caged rats consumed 20 times more morphine than the rats in rat park. To emphasize his point, he actually pre-empted some rats' entrance into Rat Park by allowing them to become addicted to the morphine while in the cages. But once the addicts were introduced to their new lives in Rat Park, they chose regular water instead of the morphine water they'd previously been addicted to.

"Nothing that we tried instilled a strong appetite for morphine or produced anything that looked like addiction in rats that were housed in a reasonably normal environment," Alexander said.

And you know what happened with the heroin-addicted Vietnam soldiers, when they returned home to their normal lives?

The exact same thing.

According to a 2012 story by NPR, the government's extensive monitoring found that 95% of soldiers stopped using heroin upon returning home to their normal environments. But how could this be? At the time, other research found that non-soldiers in America who sought treatment for heroin addiction and returned to their normal environments had a relapse rate of over 90%.

The difference between these two groups of people, in retrospect, is clear. The drug was the same. It was the change of environments for the Vietnam soldiers that was the difference. They went from a pretty hellish environment, back to a relatively normal environment. Non-soldiers who became addicted in America didn't change their environment at all. The environments drove the drug usage, not the drug itself.

And that, in my opinion, is a big part of what drives the substance abuse of our modern society. We are in cages, like the caged lab rats, and we're self-medicating. We're isolated and have little or no time to participate in our communities, or build stronger relationships with others.

As a result, our society is becoming more like the non-soldiers who had the high rate of heroin addiction, because our "work obsessed" environment isn't that enjoyable, when we have so little time for relationships and exercise and health.

But what happens when we have our time and freedom back, and we are able to have better relationships and better communities? I believe that's when we'll become more like the animals who stopped self-medicating, and more like the soldiers who returned home and immediately dropped their addictions.

Improving Happiness

The object of work is to improve quality of life. Unfortunately, today we measure quality of life too much by your level of income. Is it better if I make $50,000 per year, or $100,000 a year? Pretty much everyone would say $100,000.

But what if people begin to realize that they can get by just fine on $50,000? That quality of life becomes actually much better because you're needing to work less? That's what the prize of retirement is, after all: retirees generally earn less, and thus cut way back on their spending, but have more leisure time, and that's the goal we're taught to aspire to. The reality is you're already there if you want to be.

That shift is coming, because while nobody was apparently looking, technology has empowered us all to work less and still have a very livable salary. We've chosen to ignore that, and just work more, and spend more on stupid shit that does not make us happy. It's consumerism and the Protestant work ethic gone awry. People can afford a high quality of life, but keep working anyway, because our possessions and our job titles have become what defines us.

I believe that's going to go away in the coming years, and when it does, happiness levels will improve across our culture.

Logistics: Easing Traffic Congestion

If half of the country moves to a five-hour day, it would virtually eliminate traffic congestion. Right now the fact that the vast majority of commuters works on the 9-to-5 schedule creates a nationwide traffic jam in the mornings and evenings. We'll save even more time in the future, when it comes to the wasted hours we spend sitting in traffic.

Empowering Entrepreneurial Spirit

The way most industrious people start a business is they work a regular day job, and then go to work on their side business at night. That's how I did it, and I worked until midnight many nights, when I was planning my escape from the corporate world. After a year of running it on the side, it started to take off. Once it was making more money for me than my day job, I made the jump.

With a five-hour workday, there's an easier path for people to start their own enterprises on the side. While this may seem like a bad thing for the employer who loses that employee, it's actually good for attracting the best and brightest talent to work for you for a few years. And a few years is all you're going to get anyway, in today's society.

For our economy at large, more people starting businesses means more jobs, and a more vibrant economy. The economy is already heading in a very entrepreneurial direction, and if the five-hour workday gets widely adopted, that may be just the thing to usher in a new entrepreneurially-driven economy.

Increasing Volunteerism

People like having a purpose and mission in life. If you reduce their base work hours, volunteerism and community involvement will increase greatly, to the benefit of communities and our society. This happens when people become affluent and achieve time wealth as well. With a five-hour workday, everyone would gain this same type of affluence, and turn to charitable interests in their community.

Herein lies the productivity of a nation of people of another kind. The Jerry Smoots of the world, millions of them, will be empowered to do what they do to contribute to enhancing the quality of life of the communities around them. You can't measure this by looking at the Gross Domestic Product of a nation, but you can measure it in the quality of life of your people, and the happiness of your children within that nation.

People Are No Longer Defined By The Wrong Measures

When we reduce these working hours, free time for people will increase by at least 200% to 300%. Yes, my friends, we're not talking about a 10%, 20%, or 30% bump in leisure time during the week, but rather going from 2-3 hours of free time in the evening to over 8-9 hours of free time. You can't do much of anything in 2-3 hours, when you have to eat and do errands in there somewhere. But with 8-9 hours of free time, you can do anything you want.

This is a 10x kind of change in quality of life. It changes individual lives, which in turn changes the entire society. It will change our daily conversations. It will change everything about life as we know it. It will no longer be normal to ask "What do you do for work?," but instead, it will be about your interests. Your relationships, your creations, your adventures. The things you're passionate about.

I know it because I live this now and I've lived an extraordinary lifestyle back when I was backpacking around Australia, having the time of my life. Instead, people will ask, "What did you do last week? What did you do today? What are you going to do tonight? What movies do you like? What are your plans for tomorrow?" We'll no longer be defined by work, because we'll no longer be spending all of our waking hours at our jobs.

We will be living, and living extraordinarily.

Chapter Eleven

THE RENAISSANCE ECONOMY

OUR ECONOMY AND OUR WORLD IS READY TO ADVANCE, AND I believe that time is near. We're approaching a period of renaissance, where we'll enjoy an entirely different way of living. A happier, more present, more time-filled, more enjoyable way of living.

If we want to accelerate the arrival of this renaissance, and we want achieve this different life more quickly, then we'll need to make some different decisions now.

Henry Ford leveraged new technologies, realized gains in productivity, and decided to apply those gains in a way that would usher in the consumer economy we currently live in. More money, more time to spend it, and more economic growth by consuming the products we could now create at a faster pace than ever.

Building products faster, spending money faster. Driving an increased consumer demand that meets our increased supply of products. That's the consumer economy, and Henry Ford was instrumental in helping to build it, a century ago.

Fast forward 100 years, and we're still inside of it. The consumer economy still drives the economic growth of America, which is why some of the most-watched indicators of our economic health are based upon how optimistic consumers are about the economy.

And what happened in the past 100 years, during times when consumers didn't feel great and didn't have much money to spend? Capitalism found its solution: debt. Loans to buy things, when people didn't have all the money.

And now, this combination of consumption and excessive debt has become a cancer to its host. Consumers are now being consumed by their own debt, from the trillions in student loan debt, to high-interest car payments, to underwater mortgages. Financial chains have replaced leg chains, as we have mindlessly become modern day slaves.

We've allowed consumerism to run rampant, and people are spending everything they make (or more). We're heavily in debt, financially unhealthy, and broken-down emotionally. And yet, somehow, we are working more. We are making more money. It doesn't add up.

It's only a matter of time before people put together all of these pieces, and realize that *time* is the key to happiness. Not more money, or more possessions, or more debt, or more work. It's time that will be valued most in the future, and there will be a tipping point.

And that is when our renaissance begins. It will be a very new type of living, with a new type of economy.

The Tides Are Already Turning

The foundation for the Renaissance Economy has been building for awhile, and you can see many examples of it in today's culture.

The younger generations, especially, are valuing all the aspects of life that are not work-related. Older generations, frustrated with decades of burnout with no real wage increases, are starting to value time away from work.

People are craving time, because it's the resource we all need the most. It's a resource that most people don't have enough of. It's also a resource that fuels experiences, which are gradually becoming understood to be more important than possessions.

Thomas Gilvovich, a psychology professor at Cornell University, has studied the difference in happiness levels toward experiences, and found them to be much higher than happiness toward material possessions. In a recent interview with FastCoexist.com, he explained these findings.

> It's counterintuitive that something like a physical object that you can keep for a long time doesn't keep you as happy as long as a once-and-done experience does. Ironically, the fact that a material thing is ever present works against it, making it easier to adapt to. It fades into the background and becomes part of the new normal.
>
> But while the happiness from material purchases diminishes over time, experiences become an ingrained part of our identity. Our experiences are a bigger part of ourselves than our material goods.
>
> You can really like your material stuff. You can even think that part of your identity is connected to those things, but nonetheless they remain separate from you. In contrast, your experiences really are part of you. We are the sum total of our experiences.

Experiences—whether it's a weekly meetup with friends, or an epic vacation—are driving more happiness in us than our possessions. People are really starting to understand that, and it's driving everyone to value their time.

To deepen this effect, it's also been shown that people are

happier in the meantime, when they've got experiences they're looking forward to. That means they're going to be even happier people at work, when they've got experiences planned regularly, and the time to enjoy more of those experiences.

As a result, spending patterns are going to change. Workers are going to value money (probably up to that happiness threshold of $75,000), but from there, it's time and experiences that will matter most. People are going to spend more of their money on experiences, not material goods. If they buy material goods, they'll be the goods related to experiences. Like a stand-up paddleboard.

If you'll just give workers their time back, they're going to be much happier with the paycheck they're receiving, because it will be perceived as more than money. It's money that comes with the missing ingredient: time. This is a paycheck, but it also comes with time, and the combination of the two is what enables the ultimate driver of happiness: experiences.

Today: Spending Our Money to Get Our Time Back

Our everyday spending patterns prove that we value our time, because we spend a lot of our money on anything that will free up more time for us when we're not at work. Think of dog walking, housecleaning, fast food, online shopping, dry cleaning. There are endless examples.

But when that tipping point arrives, and we enter our renaissance, everything will change.

When we've reduced our working hours and have our entire afternoons and evenings free, it will change how we all operate on a daily basis. We'll consume everything differently and more sustainably, from the coffee we'll make at home, to the silverware we'll wash instead of throw away.

Ford believed that extra time would lead to more consumption of goods, and he was right. But I think it's going to be a bit different this time. In the Renaissance Economy, people will consume more items and services that are related to experiences, and they'll stop consuming the wasteful things that simply saved them a minute or two.

Similar to Henry Ford, my thinking about this is inspired by envisioning the future market for my company's products. I see a future where people are going to be increasing the time they spend on recreation, and the range of activities they do. As a beach lifestyle company, we're excited about that. At our core, we see ourselves as a company that builds tools for the human spirit.

We're going to benefit from people having their afternoons open to go out paddleboarding, biking, surfing, and having fun with their friends and families. And according to the happiness research, the customers who buy our products in order to experience those activities, they're going to benefit as well. It's a win-win.

This renaissance and its new economy will benefit every aspect of society, and will drive greater demand for the products and services that are related to experiences. There will be a new increase in consumption, but mostly toward the less wasteful and more sustainable products and services.

Our Money Will Go Further

Not only has technology enabled us to work more efficiently, but it's also made things less expensive. It's brought consumers and producers much closer together, and made most of the middlemen irrelevant. And that's why, if you're smart with your money, you'll find that it goes a lot further today.

As an example, take a look at our direct-to-consumer beach lifestyle website at TowerMade.com. We produce a variety of beach lifestyle products, and we produce them in some of the exact same factories as many other high-quality brands you'll find in retail stores. But there's a difference: our customers enjoy enormous savings, because we sell our products directly to them.

One hat in particular, it usually sells for $20 in retail stores, but it only costs $1.84 to produce. That $20 retail price that customers pay is literally ten times the cost, and it's because of the all the distributors, wholesalers, sales commissions, and other elements of expensive retail markup in that old school retail model.

But the world is changing, and we sell that exact same high-quality hat at a very transparent and fair markup that reflects what it actually costs us to produce and distribute that hat. As a result, our customers pay 50-75% less at TowerMade. com than they'd pay at our retail competitors, for the exact same product.

Another Way Our Money Will Go Further

In many instances, this extra time is going to reduce people's cost of living. It will lead to a less expensive life that will enable people to work less and relax more.

When we were backpacking around Australia for three months, it was amazing how inexpensive life was, when we had time to do all the little things that would've cost us money otherwise. We had time to go to the grocery store and cook our own meals.

We had time to take the slower, cheaper forms of transportation. We could take a bicycle if we wanted, or hike, or take a bus. Lodging is often cheaper as well, as we lived socially to spread the costs out, like with hostels. Better relationships mean more people are living together as couples and families, as opposed to everyone living alone. Those are the types of cost efficiencies that open up, when you have time.

We had a very sustainable and low-cost way of living in Australia, and it was *time* that unlocked all of those benefits. I spent about $7,000 to live and travel for three months, but it could've been done for half of that, really. I could've done it all for $3,500, which is closer to what the other travelers we met were spending. That same $3,500 is about what people spend on one week's vacation in today's hurried, frantic world, where we too often substitute money for time.

Vacations are expensive, because of time. When you've only got a week for vacation, your money is focused on giving you more free time. But when you've got an abundance of time, you don't need nearly as much money. You can cook, you can take public transportation, you can do so many other things that you didn't have time for before. And these same efficiencies will happen in your everyday life.

More importantly, that three-month adventure I took through Australia was much better than any vacation I could possibly buy for $50,000, because my days were spent meeting people, developing relationships, doing shared activities, and going on adventures. Is it any surprise that I woke up every day with an overwhelming feeling of gratitude? Even if I had a hangover every now and then?

You see, I wasn't trying to buy happiness. I was simply experiencing happiness, because I had all the time in the world to do just that.

Time Is the New Money

Repeat that. Time is the new money. Internalize that notion.

Enhancing the quality of life is the ultimate goal of a civilized society. Money to a certain degree can improve the quality of life, but so can time. Today, more so for time.

People trade their time for money. That's what labor, in the historical sense, has always equated to. This has made sense throughout history to trade our relatively plentiful (and renewable) resource of time, for the relatively scarce resource of money. I give you 8-10 hours a day, you give me wages which I can use to pay for my essentials of living and luxuries. The idea here is that to enhance your quality of life you have to work harder, or work more so that you can earn more money. That's what we've been taught.

But this viewpoint is only valid if we live in a society of scarcity, where it's hard to take care of your essentials. That may have been the case in America 100 years ago, but it is not the case today. The world has changed, and it's changed dramatically.

Advances in technology and the resulting advances in productivity have brought us into a world that is increasingly characterized by abundance for large swaths of our society, like knowledge workers. Providing for true essentials only takes a small percent of our income today, but we're spending more and more on luxuries. That's because marketers have convinced us that these luxuries are now our baseline essentials. But they aren't.

There is a lot of talk in America about the growing gap in income equality. This is what most people point to as the biggest problem in our country, as if we'd all be a lot happier if we were to redistribute that wealth more equally. But the thing is it's just a gap in wealth. It's just money, and that excessive wealth that the 1% is accumulating doesn't really make them any happier.

I live in a beach community in San Diego. There is a high concentration of wealth in the beach communities of Southern California. There are entire neighborhoods where you can't get a house for under $5 million, and those aren't even waterfront. Million dollar houses are commonplace throughout San Diego. My guess is there are tens of thousands of them.

In the part of town I live in, Pacific Beach, there's a mix of these expensive houses, apartments, and rentals that pack in college kids and tourists. I ride my beach cruiser along the boardwalk and I can peer into these beach pads. At many of these houses and apartments, many of them pretty crappy places, I always see a bunch of people hanging out having a good time, daytime, night time, and weekends.

But one mansion in particular has always stood out to me, because there is never anyone there enjoying it during the day, and almost every night when I ride by there's one guy in there with the lights out watching TV by himself.

I feel sorry for that lonely dude in his massive beach pad. Clearly, he's accumulated massive wealth. But that doesn't buy him friends. It doesn't buy him love, or a family. It really doesn't buy him much. In his case, it hasn't even really bought him his free time back, as I've never seen him enjoying this beach mansion during the day. Not even once in the several years I've been riding past it.

To me, this guy symbolizes a lot of where our society's objectives have gone awry. On paper, many may conclude that he is the measure of success. What I see is someone who doesn't really have a much higher quality of life than the homeless guys I'll likely encounter just a little further down the boardwalk.

Once the wealthy arrive at that point of wealth and realize that it doesn't make them any happier, you know what the smart ones inevitably do with that wealth? They figure out ways to trade their money for time. They'll spend absurd amounts of money to save time, because time is the one thing they don't have any more of than anyone else.

Private jets are really just about a very expensive way of buying your time back. VIP entrance is about skipping the line. Flying first class with a sleeper seat? Buying time because you can sleep enroute. Hiring a personal chef, or driver, or nanny? It's just about buying your time back, because that's where happiness lies: in having free time to do with as you like.

The interesting thing here, and I would argue the critical thing here, is that whether we're in the 1% or the 99%, we all have exactly the same 24 hours in each day. Yet, while regular people are acting like sheep and all trading more and more of their time for money, the smarter of the wealthy people and my most successful entrepreneurial friends (knowing that their money beyond $75,000/year isn't doing much for their happiness) are trading more and more of their money for *time*.

In our consumerism-gone-awry society, almost everyone is missing the point that time is the new money. In our era of a massively productive workforce, time is now the only true scarcity, not money.

Asking if the citizens of the US have a problem of wealth inequality is the wrong question, because we're actually looking for an answer that provides a higher collective quality of life. Yes, it seems really unfair when you consider that we're moving very quickly towards a reality that 1% of the population controls as much wealth as the other 99% combined.

That's part of the new world we live in—everything operates under a power curve. But who really cares? We're actually interested in happiness and quality of life for all people. We need to be asking if our citizens have a problem of free time inequality, because that is the true foundation of happiness and quality of life.

So, do we have a problem of time inequality? The answer to that question is a resounding yes, with the average person working 47 hours per week. We have a time inequality problem. That is the atrocity, not that some billionaires are buying $100 million homes and mega-yachts.

Addressing this time inequality is what the five-hour workday is about. Giving people back today's most precious and scarce commodity, and in doing so leveling the playing field of quality of life for a very large swath of society in a very meaningful way.

If the norm becomes that regular people are working five hours in a 24 hour day, who cares how much free time the 1% of society can buy with their massive war chests of wealth? At best, they can buy another five hours of free time than the rest of us have. We might have only a tiny percentage of the money they have, but with a five-hour workday, we'll have about 70% of the spare time they have (11 hours of free time, versus the 16 hours of free time they have).

With the five-hour workday, it is very possible for all of us to close the gap between the wealthy and the poor, in terms of *time.*

The Future Will Bring Back Our Happier Past

When the Renaissance Economy arrives, we'll finally be able to get back to where we started: focusing on life, liberty, and the pursuit of happiness. We'll be back to our healthier and happier past, when people knew that work was just a means to an end. When people worked to increase their quality of life, as opposed to what we've got now: a life full of nothing but work.

The industrial revolution, and the consumerism that followed, really put us on a hamster wheel. We became more efficient, worked a little less at first, but then we began to work more, so we could buy more. And we became more efficient again, but this time, we didn't change anything. We just kept running on that hamster wheel, working longer hours than ever, earning more than ever, and being more tired and sick and unhappy than ever.

The problem is, we haven't been meeting this core objective of work: a higher quality of life, and a happier society. We're lonely. We're divorced, or avoiding marriage entirely. Our kids are unhappy. We're addicted to prescription drugs and television sets. We are physically and mentally unhealthy.

We are in a crisis. It's a crisis that can only be solved by giving people their time back.

So let's do that. Let's step back and take the focus off of a work-focused life. Let's reposition work as the thing it was always supposed to be: the thing we did just enough of, as efficiently as possible, so that we could get back to doing all the things that drive our true happiness.

We're highly efficient now, and that's the key ingredient to the Renaissance Economy. For the first time in the history of the world, we really don't have to work that much to meet our basic needs. If we'll simply adjust our working hours, we'll unlock the possibilities of what could be done with our new abundance of time and earnings.

In the Renaissance Economy, we'll shift that time away from our workplace, and instead pursue our interests, our relationships, our physical health, and our mental health. And it will be one of the greatest eras in all of human history, because we'll have a healthy, well-adjusted society of people again.

Consumerism will be in full force, but we'll be consuming experiences, and the products that are part of those experiences. Instead of sacrificing our time to stockpile possessions, we'll be consuming our time toward the much happier pursuit of enjoyable experiences.

The New Opportunity in "After Hours" Consumption

An entirely new set of economic opportunities are going to arise for businesses that understand that there's going to be a new range of time, with services and products as a result. That chunk of time isn't just another hour or two in the evening, it's the entire afternoon. Daylight hours, with an activity-friendly window of time that will be newly opened.

It's funny, when I look back at Ford's commentary 100 years ago, it's clear that everyone was worried that free time would just lead to more drinking. It was during the time of prohibition, so it's understandable. And I don't doubt that some people would use their spare time for debauchery today, but much more so, I think they're going to do things that are healthy and beneficial for them.

I believe it's natural to focus on getting into better physical shape, if you've got a lot of time on your hands. When you know you'll have your entire days free, it's easier to get in the habits of fitness, and eating well. The two go hand in hand.

If you're a business owner, you've got plenty of incentives to help your employees become healthier. Healthier employees are happier, more productive, less absent from work, and less costly to your benefit plans. When you give people their time back, I truly believe that most of them will pursue a healthier lifestyle. That's what I see in many of the entrepreneurs that I know today, who have replaced work time with activities and habits that make them healthier.

There were futurists in the past who predicted that productivity could slow down at some point, because we'll only need a modest amount of income for everyone to have a good life. It was predicted by many that we'd only need to work 15 hours a week at that point.

I believe that it's time. We're on the doorstep of a life that we've never seen before. A nirvana, a land of abundance and opportunity, where we'll all have the freedom to pursue our happiness.

Life will no longer be about working five long days, and pursuing your happiness on the other two. No more Monday blues. No more hump days where people are yearning for the weekend. And no more TGIF.

It will be about being able to pursue your happiness every single day of your life. That's a renaissance.

The Question We Need to Ask, And Today's Wrong Answer

Right now, we're moving in the right direction, but we've got the majority of workers still unconsciously brainwashed, running on the hamster wheel of unhappiness. They're thinking that a $100,000 salary is nice, but believing that they'd be happier if they made $150,000.

They get there, and nothing changes, so they assume that it's time to go run their own business. They run their business the same way they ran their career: focused on money and growth of profits. But what is the end of this game? What's the point of it?

There's a human factor in here, and a question we need to ask right now: what is the point of this rat race we've been running? It's clearly driven by some type of greed, some type of endless hunger that is never satisfied. And it's clearly making us miserable, sick, and lonely.

And yet, we participate in this. It doesn't feel like we're willing participants, or that we have a mental choice. But that's the assumption we need to challenge. And to do so, we've got to think of this as liberating our minds. As Bob Marley sang, we've got to free ourselves from this mental slavery.

We've got to stop assuming that it makes sense to work harder and longer hours, to make more money, to buy more things. I don't necessarily think it's borne of greed. I think it's just a collective delusion of society that our lives will be improved if we make more money and work harder. But we're finding the exact opposite now, and the crisis caused by our excessive work is finally becoming obvious.

So let's ask again: what is the purpose of life, and how should work fit into that?

Let's take a more humanistic look at this. We're trying to really just increase the quality of life for ourselves, and everyone around us, right? That's our employees, our customers, our owners, our communities, our entire countries.

So how do we do things differently, in order to achieve that?

Why The "One Percent" Can't Stop This (And Eventually Won't Want To)

It's no secret that we've currently got a significant division of wealth happening in our country. I believe it comes from people being so rich that they're afraid of losing it all, and afraid of empowering their employees by sharing profits, time, or knowledge. But the truth is, this is all just fear.

Ultimately, the 1% is exactly that: 1%. They're only 1% of the people, and they can't do it without the other 99%. The majority of workers do get a say in this life, and they do get to decide what they're willing to do, and what deal they'll make for their labor. And believe me, they're about to ask for the better deal that is long overdue.

They'll start getting that better deal, from companies like mine.

And that's where this snowball will start, because not only will we prove that it improves the quality of life for everyone, but we're also proving that it makes companies more productive, profitable, and competitive.

What happened when we moved to a five-hour workday in June of 2015? Well, everything improved on our financials across the board. And this is coming from a company that was doing pretty outstanding with our 2014 numbers, as our financial performance landed us as the 239th fastest-growing company in America, after having been named the fastest-growing private company in San Diego the year prior. How did we improve upon that in the year we moved to a five-hour workday?

Here are our 2015 numbers:

- Revenue increased 42% from 2014
- Net Income as a percent of revenue increased 31% from 2014
- Expenses as a percent of revenue decreased 23% from 2014
- Payroll as a percent of revenue decreased 29% from 2014

Things are still improving. In March of 2016, Forbes published an article titled, "Ten of the Best Businesses To Come Out Of *Shark Tank*." We were listed at #6 out of 10. Rankings were measured by 2015 annual revenue. If you dig a little deeper, and look at pre-investment valuations (based on the deal made with the Sharks) compared to 2015 annual revenues (the best proxy of current valuation), we'd rank #2 on this list.

This is a pretty competitive field, yet we're nearly leading the pack now and I believe we are on track to do just that within a few years. We're working fewer hours than most people and likely seeing better results. We're doing things more efficiently, and I've given you the recipe of how to join us.

Small company by small company, this will spread nationwide. And companies like mine will continue to work circles around bigger companies, and steal their best employees, as well as their customers. The big companies will eventually follow, and when that happens, we'll find ourselves in a nation with a highly-competent, highly-productive, and highly-efficient economy.

In the short term, the 1% and the large corporations may fight the five-hour workday, out of fear. But in the end—when they understand the new levels of productivity, profitability, and employee retention—they'll join the party.

CONCLUSION

———

Believe You Can, And Take Your Leap

When I was researching the history of our eight-hour workday, there was a critical moment that opened my eyes to what was truly possible. It was the moment I finished reading about where our current eight-hour day and 40-hour week came from, and it struck me like a lightning bolt.

Holy shit, I thought. This eight-hour day was just invented out of thin air. It was just an action taken by a business owner who believed it was time to do it for his company, and for his society.

This life-changing reduction of the workday didn't start with a government order, or a religious doctrine. It started with one person who believed it was the right thing to do. But how can we possibly have the courage that Henry Ford had?

In 1994, one of the most innovative knowledge workers in the history of the world made a very powerful statement about the mindset it takes to create change:

When you grow up, you tend to get told that the world is just the way it is, and your life is just to live your life inside the world. Try not to bash into the walls too much. Try to have a nice family life, have fun, save a little money.

That's a very limited life. Life can be much broader, once you discover one simple fact, and that is—everything around you that you call life, was made up by people that were no smarter than you. And you can change it, you can influence it, you can build your own things that other people can use.

I think that's very important and however you learn that, once you learn it, you'll want to change life and make it better, cause it's kind of messed up, in a lot of ways. Once you learn that, you'll never be the same again.

That's the mindset it takes, to understand that any one of us is capable of changing the reality we see around us. And that's the mindset Steve Jobs had, when he spoke those words in 1994, before he proceeded to change the entire world with his inventions.

Removing Our Biggest Barrier

The biggest barrier is that people simply do not believe they are the person to do it. They believe it cannot be done by them, or by anyone else, because we've always worked this eight-hour day and we've just got to accept it.

Those people are wrong. We do *not* have to accept what we've done in the past. We *should* not accept it.

That's why I wanted to write this book. In some ways I feel as if my unique experiences in life lead me to this point. I've lived a life less ordinary. I want to show you that it's possible, and it's working, and you can do this too. I want to take our experiment and its success, and make it public. I want you to try this for yourself and your company, and improve upon it further.

If you own a company, or if you have a way to communicate with the person who owns the company you work for, then you can make this decision. You can stand up and say, hey, I think this is worth a test. I think this might drive more productivity, and be a huge attractor of talented workers, and retain the talented ones we've got.

You can be the first to push the needle at your company. Someone has to initiate the conversation, or the conversation will never happen. You don't have to be the first company in America to do this. We've jumped off the cliff and tested the depth. The water's fine. There's nothing to fear. The sky didn't fall. Our processes got better. We're still growing fast.

But now, we're growing in a stronger, more sustainable, happier way. That's what you can look forward to, if you'll take this leap of faith.

Your Magic Bullet: Temporary Experimentation

The eight-hour workday was just invented by one business owner, using what limited data was available to him a century ago. But today, we have much more information. We can design something better, if we will simply trust this new information.

I realize that facts about increased productivity aren't enough. Decisions like this one require our emotions to be aligned with the facts. We need to have confidence, and reduce our fears.

We're afraid of change. We're afraid we'll fail. It comforts us, to listen to the skeptical voice in our head that tells us a five-hour workday is crazy, and that an eight-hour workday is how it's always been, and always should be.

These are the mental hurdles we have to jump over, to win the race ahead. And I've got the perfect solution that will help you jump those hurdles: a three-month experiment.

When we did our initial experiment, it was during the summer. Summer is a great season for try a five-hour workday, because the summer days are long and sunny, and it's a time when people can really make the most of their newly-free afternoons and evenings.

Final Steps: How To Begin Your Experiment

Here's exactly how to begin the experiment, in the way that gives it the highest chance of succeeding.

Gather your team at the beginning of the day, and explain that you're doing an experiment in productivity by shortening the working hours. We'll just call it a summer schedule, so everyone expects it to end in the fall. This puts less pressure on it for everyone, makes it appear temporary, and gives your company a path back to the eight-hour workday in case it doesn't work.

At this point, there might already be a buzz of positive energy in the air. The employees might be cheering already. This is the point where it's important to clarify the most important aspect of the experiment: we've got to find a way to accomplish all of our tasks in five hours.

Now, both sides of the deal are disclosed. Employees get time, the company gets productivity, and everybody wins. That makes this experiment logical and trustworthy, which is important.

When you explain that everybody is expected to have the same level of productivity and output that they had before, but they need to get it done by 1:00 p.m., their minds are going to start finding ways to do that. They're going to work miracles. They'll figure out creative solutions to accomplish it. Why?

Because after a lifetime of working long hours, they finally have a great incentive to be more productive: they get to go home. They keep their job, keep their paychecks, but gain their time. It's a powerful incentive.

You can't get the productivity gains if you don't reduce the hours. If you instead just asked everyone to try to finish their work a little faster, they've got zero incentive to examine processes and find creative solutions. You haven't changed the stakes in a way that matters to *them*. And you haven't implemented the time constraints that will encourage innovation.

But when you say, "Alright, for the next three months, I want everybody done with their work and out the door at 1:00 p.m.," then you've really changed the game. Now you've implemented the time constraint that will force creative thinking and inspire innovation. This is why every single company on the planet could benefit from shortened workdays.

Even if you don't choose to adopt a five-hour workday permanently, there are plenty of short-term benefits. In the worst case scenario, you will have spent three months stretching everyone's mind to think about how to become more efficient. How to use new technologies and processes to get eight hours of work finished in five hours. Imagine the benefit you will realize just from that.

Additionally, for three glorious months, your employees are going to experience a happier life. They're going to be happier at work, and happier at home. If they were thinking about leaving your company, maybe they'll decide to stay. They'll tell their friends, who tell their friends. You'll get some talented people bringing you ideas for your business, hoping to get the five-hour day they heard about.

That's your worst-case scenario. Doesn't sound too bad at all, does it?

If you're in a small company, it's easy to try this experiment. But what if you're in a huge company? If you're in a bigger company, I understand how change can be more difficult. It can feel like you're trying to turn a barge, instead of a canoe.

But you've got this book, right? Pass it around. See if you can start a conversation with someone else at work, and possibly seed a groundswell of interest around you.

Everybody in every company has a little influence, if they

simply communicate with each other. If you're in upper management, then you can really push through something like this, and doing it as an experiment takes away the typical pressure and risk that comes along with a decision like this.

Whether you're the business owner, a middle manager, or the newest employee, this is a very real opportunity for you to be a hero.

Think about it: if this works, every single person in your company—from the owners to the employees—will remember that this was your idea. They'll remember that it was your idea and your innovative thinking that changed their lives and the company for the better.

And you know what feels even better than other people seeing you as heroic?

Looking into the mirror, every day, and seeing it in yourself. Seeing someone who has the courage to emancipate their mind from mental slavery. Someone who believes in themselves as much as Steve Jobs did.

Seeing someone who is mentally and physically healthy. Someone who is overflowing with energy, friends, family, love, and happiness.

And best of all, seeing someone who has the afternoon off. Every single day of their life.

So I'll see you at the beach?

Bring your paddle board. The waves are going to be amazing today.

✳   ✳   ✳

For more resources and updates on the five-hour workday at our company and others, please visit us at www.FiveHourWorkDay.com. We'll update everyone from time to time on how our experiment is progressing, and how other companies are innovating as well.

Use #5HourWorkDay on social media to tag pics of you enjoying life after 1:00 p.m. during the week!

Additionally, please feel free to email me at Stephan@ towerpaddleboards.com with ideas or success stories regarding productivity experiments at your company.

Thanks for reading my book!

ACKNOWLEDGMENTS

First and foremost, I'd like to thank my amazing editor, Brad Kauffman, for pouring his heart and soul into this book. Brad went above and beyond to do a ton of research and add critical pieces where we needed them. While I'm the only one listed as the author on this book, Brad added so much that I feel like he really almost co-authored this with me.

I'd also like to give a special thanks to Keating Coffey, who was instrumental in constructing the framework of this book. Without Keating's magic touch, this is all just rambling thoughts. And none of this happens without my brilliant and efficient team of publishing managers including: Andrew Lynch, Zach Obront, and Jeremy Brown.

ABOUT THE AUTHOR

STEPHAN AARSTOL is the CEO and Founder of Tower Paddle Boards, an online, manufacturer-direct brand in the stand up paddle boarding industry. With a three-year growth rate of 1853%, Tower was named the Fastest Growing Company in San Diego by the *San Diego Business Journal*, and was featured in the 2015 Inc. 500 List of America's Fastest Growing Companies.

After appearing on ABC's *Shark Tank* and securing an investment from Mark Cuban, Stephan was featured by *People Magazine* as one of "*Shark Tank*'s Biggest Winners." Stephan's company quickly became one of Mark Cuban's best-performing investments from the popular show, and in early 2016, ABC returned to feature Tower Paddle Boards in a nationally-televised episode of *Beyond the Tank*.

Tower began as a disruptive, direct-to-consumer stand up

paddle board company, and has since evolved into a more holistic beach lifestyle company. Today, Tower offers a growing array of beach lifestyle products, sold and shipped directly to consumers at a fraction of traditional retail prices. Tower's successful brand extensions include a beach lifestyle magazine, *Tower Magazine* (online at Tower.Life), a sunglass company at (SunglassesBy-Tower.com), and a direct-to-consumer surf and beach lifestyle company (online at TowerMade.com).

Stephan's objective is to build Tower into the world's premiere beach lifestyle brand, and he currently has plans to extend the Tower brand into many additional business units.

As an entrepreneurial thought leader and online marketing expert, Stephan's insights have been published in the *Washington Post, Inc., Forbes, Entrepreneur, Fast Company, Mashable*, and many other prominent business publications.